T&T CLARK STUDY GUIDES TO THE OLD TESTAMENT

Proverbs: Wisdom Calls

Series Editor
Adrian Curtis, University of Manchester, UK
Published in association with the Society for Old Testament Study

T0285144

Other titles in the series include:

T & T CLARK STUDY GUIDES TO THE NEW TESTAMENT:

Proverbs: Wisdom Calls

An Introduction and Study Guide

Zoltán Schwáb

t&t clark

LONDON • NEW YORK • OXFORD • NEW DELHI • SYDNEY

T&T CLARK
Bloomsbury Publishing Plc
50 Bedford Square, London, WC1B 3DP, UK
1385 Broadway, New York, NY 10018, USA
29 Earlsfort Terrace, Dublin 2, Ireland

BLOOMSBURY, T&T CLARK and the T&T Clark logo are
trademarks of Bloomsbury Publishing Plc

First published in Great Britain 2023

A catalogue record for this book is available from the British Library.

Library of Congress Cataloging-in-Publication Data
Names: Schwáb, Zoltán S., author.
Title: Proverbs : wisdom calls : an introduction and study guide / by Zoltán Schwáb.
Description: London ; New York : T&T Clark, 2023. | Series: T&T Clark's study guides to
the Old Testament | Includes bibliographical references and index. |
Summary: "Introduces the Book of Proverbs, examining its characteristics,
historical context and key themes, and encouraging existential engagement with
Proverbs"– Provided by publisher.
Identifiers: LCCN 2022050760 (print) | LCCN 2022050761 (ebook) |
ISBN 9781350187863 (paperback) | ISBN 9781350187870 (hardback) |
ISBN 9781350187887 (epub) | ISBN 9781350187894 (pdf)
Subjects: LCSH: Bible. Proverbs–Criticism, interpretation, etc.
Classification: LCC BS1465.52 .S388 2023 (print) | LCC BS1465.52 (ebook) |
DDC 223/.706–dc23/eng/20230323
LC record available at https://lccn.loc.gov/2022050760
LC ebook record available at https://lccn.loc.gov/2022050761

ISBN: HB: 978-1-3501-8787-0
       PB: 978-1-3501-8786-3
       ePDF: 978-1-3501-8789-4
       eBook: 978-1-3501-8788-7

Series: T&T Clark's Study Guides to the Old Testament

Typeset by Integra Software Services Pvt. Ltd.
Printed and bound in Great Britain

To find out more about our authors and books visit www.bloomsbury.com
and sign up for our newsletters.

Contents

Series preface

How can a potential reader be sure that a guide to a biblical book is balanced and reliable? One answer is, 'If the guide has been produced under the auspices of an organization such as the Society for Old Testament Study.'

Founded in 1917, the Society for Old Testament Study (or SOTS as it is commonly known) is a British and Irish society for Old Testament scholars, but with a worldwide membership. It seeks to foster the academic study of the Old Testament/Hebrew Bible in various ways, for example, by arranging conferences (usually twice per year) for its members, maintaining links with other learned societies with similar interests in the British Isles and abroad, and producing a range of publications, including scholarly monographs, and collections of essays by individual authors or on specific topics. Periodically it has published volumes seeking to provide an overview of recent developments and emphases in the discipline at the time of publication. The annual Society for Old Testament Study Book List, containing succinct reviews by members of the Society of works on the Old Testament and related areas which have been published in the previous year or so, has proved an invaluable bibliographical resource.

With the needs of students in particular in mind, the Society also produced a series of study guides to the books of the Old Testament. This first series of Old Testament guides, published for the Society by Sheffield Academic Press in the 1980s and 1990s, under the general editorship of the late Professor Norman Whybray, was well received as a very useful resource which teachers could recommend to their students with confidence. But it has inevitably become dated with the passage of time, hence the decision that a new series should be commissioned.

The aim of the new series is to continue the tradition established by the first Series, namely to provide a concise, comprehensive, manageable and affordable guide to each biblical book. The intention is that each volume will contain an authoritative overview of the current thinking on the traditional matters of Old Testament/Hebrew Bible introduction, addressing matters of content, major critical issues and theological perspectives, in the light of recent scholarship, and suggesting suitable further reading. Where appropriate to the particular biblical book or books, attention may also be given to less traditional approaches or particular theoretical perspectives.

All the authors are members of the Society, known for their scholarship and with wide experience of teaching in universities and colleges. The series general editor, Adrian Curtis, taught Old Testament/Hebrew Bible at the University of Manchester for many years, is a former secretary of the Society and was president of the Society for 2016.

It is the hope of the Society that these guides will stimulate in their readers an appreciation of the body of literature whose study is at the heart of all its activities.

Abbreviations

AB	Anchor Bible
ABS	Archaeology and Biblical Studies
AHEJ	*Archaeology and History of Eighth-Century Judah*, edited by Z. I. Farber and J. L. Wright. Atlanta: SBL Press.
AIL	Ancient Israel and Its Literature
ANEM	Ancient Near East Monographs
BAS	Bible in Africa Studies
BBR	*Bulletin for Biblical Research*
BETL	Bibliotheca ephemeridum theologicarum lovaniensium
BIS	Biblical Interpretation Series
BKAT	Biblischer Kommentar: Altes Testament
BSac	Bibliotheca Sacra
BTA	Bible and Theology in Africa
BZAW	Beihefte zum *ZAW*
CBQ	*Catholic Biblical Quarterly*
CBQMS	*Catholic Biblical Quarterly*, Monograph Series
CCBWL	*Cambridge Companion to Biblical Wisdom Literature*, edited by K. J. Dell, S. R. Millar and A. J. Keefer. Cambridge: Cambridge University Press.
CDLI	*Cuneiform Digital Library Initiative*. 2022. (https://cdli.ucla.edu/search/search_results.php?SearchMode=Text&ObjectID=P497322)
CISW	*Contextualizing Israel's Sacred Writings: Ancient Literacy, Orality, and Literary Production*, edited by B. B. Schmidt. Atlanta: SBL Press.
FAT	Forschungen zum Alten Testament

FRLANT	Forschungen zur Religion und Literatur des Alten und Neuen Testaments
HS	*Hebrew Studies*
HTS TSTS	*HTS Teologiese Studies/Theological Studies*
JBL	*Journal of Biblical Literature*
JETS	*Journal of the Evangelical Theological Society*
JSOT	*Journal for the Study of the Old Testament*
JSOTSup	*Journal for the Study of the Old Testament*, Supplement Series
JTI	*Journal of Theological Interpretation*
LHBOTS	Library of Hebrew Bible/Old Testament Studies
MBSS	McMaster Biblical Studies Series
NBS	Numen Book Series
OBO	Orbis Biblicus et Orientalis
OHWB	*Oxford Handbook of Wisdom and the Bible*, edited by W. Kynes. New York: Oxford University Press.
OHWHB	*Oxford Handbook of the Writings of the Hebrew Bible*, edited by D. F. Morgan. New York: Oxford University Press.
OTE	*Old Testament Essays*
PHOE	*The Problem of the Hexateuch and Other Essays, by Gerhard von Rad.* Edinburgh: Oliver & Boyd.
PIW	*Perspectives on Israelite Wisdom: Proceedings of the Oxford Old Testament Seminar.* LHBOTS 618. Edited by J. Jarick. London, New York, Oxford, New Delhi, Sydney: T&T Clark.
PSAT	Poetologische Studien zum Alten Testament
RB	*Revue Biblique*
SBLDS	Society of Biblical Literature, Dissertation Series
RBS	Resources for Biblical Study
RPI	*Reading Proverbs Intertextually.* Library of Hebrew Bible/Old Testament Studies 629. Edited by K. J. Dell and W. Kynes. London, New York, Oxford, New Delhi, Sydney: T&T Clark.

SBLSym   Society of Biblical Literature Symposium Series

SIW   *'See, I will bring a scroll recounting what befell me' (Ps 40:8): Epigraphy and Daily Life from the Bible to the Talmud,* edited by E. Eshel and Y. Levin. Göttingen: Vandenhoeck & Ruprecht.

SJT   *Scottish Journal of Theology*

SOW   *Seeking Out the Wisdom of the Ancients: Essays Offered to Honor Michael V. Fox on the Occasion of His Sixty-Fifth Birthday,* edited by R. L. Troxel, K. G. Friebel and D. R. Magary. Winona Lake: Eisenbrauns.

SPAW   Sitzungsberichte der preussischen Akademie der Wissenschaften

SWIHB   *Second Wave Intertextuality and the Hebrew Bible.* RBS 93. Edited by M. Grohmann and H. C. P. Kim. Atlanta: SBL Press.

TOTC   Tyndale Old Testament Commentaries

TSAJ   Texts and Studies in Ancient Judaism

VT   *Vetus Testamentum*

VTSup   *Vetus Testamentum,* Supplements

WBC   Word Biblical Commentary

WBCWL   *Wiley Blackwell Companion to Wisdom Literature,* edited by S. L. Adams and M. Goff. Hoboken, NJ; Chichester: John Wiley & Sons Ltd.

WMANT   Wissenschaftliche Monographien zum Alten und Neuen Testament

WTWT   *Was There a Wisdom Tradition? New Prospects in Israelite Wisdom Studies.* AIL 23. Edited by M. R. Sneed. Atlanta: SBL Press.

WYAMS   *Wisdom, You Are My Sister: Studies in Honor of Roland E. Murphy, O.Carm., on the Occasion of His Eightieth Birthday.* CBQMS 29. Edited by M. L. Barré. Washington: The Catholic Biblical Association of America.

ZAW   *Zeitschrift für die alttestamentliche Wissenschaft*

ZTK   *Zeitschrift für Theologie und Kirche*

Introduction

In a popular textbook about biblical interpretation, Grant Osborne provides the following advice to his students: 'if anyone is half asleep and does not hear a question that I ask, there is a 50 per cent chance of being correct if he or she answers, "context"' (Osborne 2006: 39). Indeed, a text can only be understood within its context. But which context? The historical context of the author, the literary context of the text and the context of the reader may lead to different interpretations. For a long time, the 'holy grail' of academic interpretation was the historical context. Once we knew who wrote a text, when and why, we knew what it said. That time is past. Literary and reader-response approaches have joined historical-critical ones. Sometimes different interpretations live in harmony even within individual minds, but there are times when they become fierce enemies. The interpretation of Proverbs is not immune to the issue of multiple contexts. For example, how should we explain the figure of Wisdom in chapter 8? Should we compare her to ancient Near Eastern goddesses (the context of ancient Near Eastern aretologies, praises of divine figures), take her to be the clever motivational rhetoric of a young boy's father (the context of chapters 1–9), as a veiled depiction of Christ (the context of the Christian canon), or as a projection of male fantasy (the context of gender interests)?

As if things were not complicated enough, our understanding of the historical, literary and canonical contexts of Proverbs and the ideological contexts of its readers is changing rapidly. Therefore, the interpretation of Proverbs is in a state of flux. I will try to do justice to this turbulent situation by taking the different contexts one by one.

Outline

Part I discusses the historical and social background of Proverbs. In Part II, which is the longest, I discuss the book's literary context. First, I provide a short commentary, highlighting some noteworthy features of the text and scholarly debates regarding key passages. I also discuss how the individual sayings, which appear mainly in chapters 10–31, should be interpreted. This discussion can be found between my notes on chapters 1–9 and 10–31. There is also an introduction to the world view of Proverbs at the end of Part II.

Parts III and IV are shorter. They focus on the canonical context of Proverbs and the context of contemporary readers, respectively. These parts are selective, giving only a taste of the issues.

Limitations

Textual variants will be largely ignored throughout the discussion. Therefore, let me say a few words about them here. The Greek Septuagint differs from the traditional (Masoretic) Hebrew text in its order (Prov. 1.1–24.22; 30.1-14; 24.23-34; 30.15–31.9; 25.1–29.27; 31.10-31). It sometimes seems to translate a different Hebrew text and it often adds new verses. It also tends to disambiguate sayings that may be open to various interpretations in the Hebrew. The Syriac is dependent on the Septuagint, and the Aramaic is dependent on the Syriac. The Vulgate follows a Hebrew that is similar to ours, but it also uses the Septuagint. The notes and examples in Fox (2015a:35–75) provide an excellent introduction to these versions (see also Clifford 1997).

The guided reading is inevitably selective. For example, translation issues are seldom mentioned. I focus on matters of interpretation that are fiercely debated, have theological importance or contribute to the interpretation of the book as a whole.

The reception history of Proverbs also falls outside the scope of this book. The reader is directed to Furey et al. (2009) and the fast-growing resource Visual Commentary on Scripture (n.d.). It may also be worth searching for related topics in blogs on biblical art (such as Anon n.d.; Jones 2015; Tali n.d.). Works on Proverbs in social media or the political public arena are yet to be written (but see the entertainingly rewritten proverbs in Greenberg 2017a, 2017b).

Translations, language and references

Biblical quotations are my translations unless noted otherwise. Readers are recommended to have the Bible in their own language in hand and if they can read the Hebrew original, they are encouraged to do so.

Proverbs with a capital 'P' refers to the book, while 'proverbs' means short sayings. Instead of using inclusive language, I will use 'son' and 'father' when translating the equivalent Hebrew terms. However, when referring to the readers of Proverbs, I will use inclusive language. The divine name is written as YHWH. I do not use an academic system to transliterate Hebrew words as my readers may be unfamiliar with such systems. Those who know Hebrew should be able to identify the words easily. 'Israelite' applies to both Israel and Judah (occasionally even to Yehud, the Persian province of Judah) or to at least one of them when we are uncertain which one is meant.

As the previous volume on Proverbs in the Old Testament Guides series was published in 1995, I focus on works in English that have been published since then. However, I also refer to older classics or foreign language works whose influence is still significant. If a foreign language work has an English translation, I refer to that. At the end of each of the four parts I highlight selected works to help readers continue their studies. More detailed guidance can be gleaned from the in-text references and the bibliography.

Biblical passages are often discussed in more than one place; therefore readers are advised to check the index when looking for a certain passage.

Selected commentaries on Proverbs

Short commentaries (up to 400 pages)

Bellis 2018: A gender-sensitive commentary. Its comments on translation issues are accessible to readers with limited knowledge of Hebrew.

Clifford 1999: The historical introduction is clearly written and the book offers a concise, insightful verse-by-verse commentary.

Davis 2000: A brief commentary on selected passages with deep spiritual reflections.

Lucas 2015: The breadth of this commentary is impressive; it provides an up-to-date introduction to the historical background and pays attention to theological and contemporary concerns.

Murphy 1998: Written by the doyen of wisdom studies in the twentieth century, this summarizes the results of a long life spent studying Proverbs.

Treier 2011: An openly Christian theological commentary.

Van Leeuwen 1997: Brief textual notes are combined with insightful theological reflections.

Detailed commentaries

Fox 2000, 2009: This masterly two-volume commentary provides thoughtful comments on each verse, detailed notes on textual variants and essays on themes and debated issues. If I could take only one commentary on Proverbs to a desert island, this would be it.

Loader 2014: Along with discussions on translation and exegesis, it pays attention to reception history. Second volume was published in 2022.

Longman 2006: Rejects the trend of looking for clusters of proverbs. It also contains twenty-eight topical studies (from 'alcohol' to 'women').

Schipper 2019a: This masterfully detailed commentary argues that Proverbs offers two levels of teaching, one for the beginner and another for the advanced scribe, and that Proverbs has more connections with Deuteronomy than usually acknowledged. Second volume is yet to be published.

Waltke 2004, 2005: This detailed two-volume commentary argues for the antiquity of Proverbs and seeks to identify clusters of proverbs.

Waltke and De Silva 2021: An abridged, updated version of Waltke's commentary.

Part I

The historical context

In many ways, Proverbs is out of joint within the biblical canon. It has linguistic oddities (Rendsburg 2016), little or no interest in Israel's history and cult and, while it contains hundreds of proverbs, none is quoted even once in other biblical books. Four different explanations have been suggested for this: (1) the authors were a distinct group of people with a distinct ideology within Israel; (2) Proverbs was written at a different time than most biblical books; (3) Proverbs was written in a different location than most biblical books; (4) Proverbs represents a distinct mode of expression. The first three options concern the historical context of the book. This is the topic of Part I (for the fourth option, see Part III).

For a long time, mainly two rival versions of explanation (1) were used to account for Proverbs' oddities. Some argued that, unlike other biblical books, its sayings had a folk origin. Others, on the other hand, thought that Proverbs was written by an elite group of sages who were different from the priests and prophets who were the authors of many other biblical books. This approach has not run out of supporters but it has been challenged in recent decades, not least due to the work of David M. Carr and Karel van der Toorn (Carr 2005, 2011; van der Toorn 2007), who have argued that all biblical books, including Proverbs, are the products of the 'scribal culture', and as such, the authors of Proverbs were not sociologically or ideologically so different from other biblical authors. If explanation (1) is ruled out, (2), (3) and (4) become more likely. Carr, for example, argues that Proverbs' unique features can be explained by its early date (which is a version of explanation (2), Carr 2011), while Rendsburg thinks that parts of Proverbs were produced by the scribes of the Northern Kingdom and the material was transferred to Judah after the Assyrian occupation of Israel (explanation (3), Rendsburg 2016).

Due to these debates, there is a bewildering array of opinions about the social and historical context of Proverbs. Part I attempts to highlight the most important views.

Social context

The scribal school

As I pass through my incarnations in every age and race,
I make my proper prostrations to the Gods of the Market Place.
Peering through reverent fingers I watch them flourish and fall,
And the Gods of the Copybook Headings, I notice, outlast them all.

(Kipling 1919)

In the opening lines of *The Gods of the Copybook Headings*, Rudyard Kipling compared ever-changing ideologies, the 'Gods of the Market Place', with the stable 'Gods of the Copybook Headings'. In his Edwardian England, the school practice of copying out proverbs written at the top of copybook pages served two purposes: to practise handwriting and to instil moral character. Kipling's point is that while fashionable ideologies come and go, old maxims are enduring. That 'dogs return to their vomit and fools to their folly' (see Prov. 26.11) was equally true three thousand years ago and today.

The pedagogical copying method predated Kipling's time. The first written proverbs have been dated to approximately 2600–2550 BCE (Alster 1997: xvi, xxi), not long after the birth of writing. There are master copies of these Sumerian proverbs in the confidently crafted cuneiform signs of teachers, accompanied by students' shaky copies (Schniedewind 2019:37, 120; Veldhuis 2000). Just like Edwardian children, Sumerians were helped by copying proverbs to master writing, tradition and morals (Carr 2005:31–2; for a similar practice in Egypt, see p. 76).

We know from the book of Sirach that proverbs were used in second century BCE Israelite scribal education. The same was true throughout the ancient Near East (Schipper 2019a:14–17; for pre-Israelite Canaanite scribes, see van der Toorn 2007), so it is reasonable to assume that proverbs continuously formed part of Israelite scribal education, including the monarchy and Persian Yehud and that we should search for the social context of the book of Proverbs in this educational system.

While in Edwardian England many people learned how to write using copybooks, in ancient Israel only the scribes may have had this privilege (Rollston 2018:458). But their number was not insignificant. The Bible refers to many of them. Shemaiah (1 Chron. 24.6) and Seraiah (2 Sam. 8.17; 20.25; 1 Chron. 18.16), his sons, Elihoreph and Ahijah (1 Kgs 4.3), Shebnah (2 Kgs 18.18; 19.2), Shaphan (2 Kgs 22.12), Elishama (Jer. 36.12) and Jonathan (Jer. 37.15, 20) were royal scribes. Jeremiah complains about scribes distorting the Torah (Jer. 8.8), but he himself used the service of a scribe, Baruch (Jer. 36.1-8), whose brother, Seriah, may have been another royal scribe (Jer. 51.59-64). Scribes are also mentioned in passing in Judges 5.14 and 1 Chronicles 2.55. Ezra 2.55, depending on the translation, might even refer to a female scribe. Presumably the word 'recorder' (*mazkir*) also denotes scribes but with the special responsibility of writing court annals (2 Sam. 8.16; 1 Kgs 4.3; 2 Kgs 18.18; Isa. 36.3; see Blenkinsopp 1995a:30; Goff 2020:197; Perdue 2008:66–7). A 'scribal chamber' is mentioned in Jeremiah 36.12 and titles such as 'the scribe of the king' (2 Kgs 12.10 [H:12:11]; 2 Chron. 24.11; see Esth. 3.12; 8.9) and 'scribe of the commander of the army' (2 Kgs 25.19; Jer. 52.25) suggest heads of contingents of scribes (Rollston 2015:79).

Archaeological finds also suggest the presence of many scribes. Abecedaries from Izbet Ṣarta (twelfth century BCE), Kuntillet 'Ajrud (ninth or eighth century BCE), Lachish (eighth and sixth centuries BCE), Arad (tenth to seventh centuries BCE), Deir 'Alla (late ninth to early eighth centuries BCE) and Kadesh Barnea (eighth or seventh century BCE) might have been intended for the writing exercises of scribal students (Davies 1995:204, 206, 210; Schniedewind 2019:23). Many seals designate their owners as scribes (van der Toorn 2007:52). Inscriptions in fortresses, administrative centres and domestic quarters (Naʾaman 2015); *ostraca* (potsherds that were used for writing notes) with ink writing (Lemaire 2015:30–1; Naʾaman 2015:62, 64; Richey 2021:35) and thousands of stamps on jar handles from Hezekiah's time (Lipschits 2018:338) testify to widespread scribal activity. Sadly, the hundreds of surviving *bullae* originally attached to papyrus documents that have perished indicate that most of the scribal activity in ancient Israel is now lost to our sight (Naʾaman 2015:50–1, 63, 65; Richey 2021:34–6; Rollston 2010:47–82, 2018:466).

Writing had become remarkably standardized by the ninth century BCE (van der Toorn 2007:89), suggesting there was an educational system with a unified curriculum (Rollston 2015, 2018:462, 469; but contrast Sanders 2009:130–3, who thinks that standardization did not necessarily require centralized education). The gradual increase of epigraphic material from the eighth to sixth century BCE (Lemaire 2015:33–4; Na'aman 2015:60–6; Rollston 2018:463–9; Whisenant 2015:152–3) suggests a growing demand for educated scribes. Therefore, numerous interpreters have held that parts of Proverbs, or perhaps all of it, were included in the standardized scribal curriculum (for example Heckl 2015:235; Lemaire 1981; Schipper 2019a:39–40; Scott 1974:3).

Scholars have identified many features of Proverbs that allegedly indicate a school setting, for example, the prologue (1.1-7) 'unambiguously presents the book ... as promoting learning' (Goff 2020:195). The admonitions to a 'son', the typical word for a pupil in the ancient Near East (Schipper 2019a:14) and the use of acrostic poems (31.10-31) would also fit a school (van der Toorn 2007:116). References to buying wisdom (4.5, 7; 16.16; 17.16; 23.23) may denote paying a tuition fee (Crenshaw 1998a:96–7; Davies 1995:199–200). When 5.13 refers to 'those who taught me', it may mean professional teachers (Davies 1995:200; Schipper 2019a:208).

Therefore, the wider ancient Near Eastern context, the many scribes mentioned in the Bible, the presence of writing in the archaeological record and many characteristics of Proverbs suggest that the book was used in scribal education. Like Edwardian students, ancient Israelite pupils copied proverbs and, in accordance with the didactic methods of the time, listened to their teachers reciting the book and memorized long sections of it (see the admonitions to incline ears, listen and write 'on the tablet of your heart', for example, 3.3; 6.21; 7.3; Carr 2005:126–8).

There is one slight problem with this conclusion. There is no surviving text or archaeological find that undisputedly refers to schools in Israel before Ben Sira in the second century BCE (and even that reference is debated, see Carr 2005:201). But this need not destroy the theory. School buildings may have existed even if we have not found them yet. Also, education may not have been dependent upon purpose-built schools and full-time teachers. It may also have happened in the apprenticeship model, when a master scribe had several pupils and taught them in buildings that served other purposes as well (Carr 2005:12–13, 20–1, 113; Schniedewind 2019:47–8). Scholarship has suggested three main possible contexts for education: the temple, the palace and the home.

The temple school

Scribal education, especially in the first millennium BCE in the ancient Near East, often took place in temples (Carr 2005:79, 83; van der Toorn 2007:56, 68, 88). Some biblical passages also associate scribes with priests

(2 Sam. 8.17; 1 Kgs 4.4; 2 Kgs 12.2). In Arad, the remains of a royal temple contained many *ostraca*, suggesting that writing was part of temple life (Na'aman 2015:63). All these comparative, biblical and archaeological pieces of evidence point to the temple as the institutional home of education. In 1955 Sigmund Mowinckel argued:

> There is every reason to believe that the school for scribes in Jerusalem, as elsewhere in the Orient, was closely connected with the temple … The guilds of scribes and temple singers and poets were closely connected.
>
> (1955:207)

More recently, van der Toorn has suggested that the scribal expertise necessary for composing books such as Proverbs resided in the temple (van der Toorn 2007:82–104). He thinks that this is corroborated by Jeremiah 18.18, where sages (fully trained scribes, according to van der Toorn) are mentioned with two groups of religious professionals, priests and prophets (2007:95).

Van der Toorn hypothesizes that these temple-scholars were responsible for writing documents that later generations of scribes formed into biblical books when Hellenism arrived with its new culture of books and reading (2007:99, 259). By the time Proverbs was being given its final form, many people could read, so although the editors were reusing material that was originally created for scribal education, they probably also had a lay readership in mind (2007:252).

However, while not denying that scribes had a role in the temple, other scholars point out that the available epigraphic material from Israel typically concerns military or economic issues without religious content (Rollston 2015:93; Schniedewind 2019:39, 310). This suggests that we should search for the scribal school in the palace.

The palace school

The Hebrew term *sopher* (scribe) evokes counting besides writing and as such reflects the bureaucratic function of scribes. Bureaucracy, then as now, was nowhere more important than in state administration. International relations also required the service of scribes who spoke foreign languages and could write diplomatic letters (Crenshaw 1998a:281; Perdue 2008:49–50). Although it is possible that the state only hired such scribes from the temple, if scribes were so important to the palace, it is natural to assume they were trained there. In the archaeological evidence, epigraphic material is often found in royal fortresses, such as Arad and Lachish, which again suggests that scribes were primarily employed by the palace (Na'aman 2015:62; Schniedewind 2019:311).

Most of the scribes mentioned in the Bible were royal scribes. King Solomon and his royal bureaucracy (1 Kgs 4.1-28) are associated with wisdom and the use of proverbs (1 Kgs 4.29-34). Proverbs' frequent mentions of kings as authors or patrons (1.1; 10.1; 25.1; 31.1) suggest that the book's provenance was in the palace (Schniedewind 2004:75–81). Many other verses refer to rulers, kings and a royal court (8.15-16; 14.28, 35; 16.10, 12-15; 17.7; 19.6, 10, 12; 20.8, 26, 28; 21.1; 22.11; 24.21-22; 25.2-7, 15; 28.2-3, 12, 15-16, 28; 29.2, 4, 12, 14, 26; 31.1-9) and presuppose a reader 'who can stand before kings' (22.29) or 'eat with a ruler' (23.1). Ansberry suggests that Proverbs has such an aristocratic flavour because it was created as a scribal training manual for future courtiers (Ansberry 2011).

Perhaps, however, we should not separate the contexts of palace and temple too strictly. These two institutions may have joined forces in order to educate scribes (Rollston 2015:93; van der Toorn 2007:84–5). Others go even further, suggesting that focusing on a combination of the temple and palace is still too restrictive. We should move beyond their precincts into humble homes if we want to understand the social context of Proverbs.

The home school

In Egypt and Mesopotamia scribal education sometimes happened in families (Golka 1983:264–5). In ancient Near Eastern archaeological records, 127 archives have been found in official buildings, but 'nearly twice as many …, 253, were associated with private houses' (Schniedewind 2015:310). Certain values and skills promoted in Proverbs (diligent work, avoiding quarrels and so on) are not specific to life in the temple or court. The temple is not even mentioned in Proverbs. Kings are mentioned, but this does not prove much. The fact that royal sayings were retained in post-monarchic times suggests that they sounded relevant to a nation which no longer had a royal court (Millar 2020:26, 162). Therefore, the search for a school only in the temple or palace may be missing the obvious: Proverbs speaks predominantly about another context – the family.

Israelite smiths, shepherds and musicians probably learned their craft from their parents. Scribal education may have worked in the same way (Carr 2005:129–30). In scribal families, knowledge could be passed on from one generation to the next (Proverbs 4.1-4 describes this process). Perhaps other boys joined such families to learn scribal knowledge and the master scribes took over the role of a father for the duration of their training (Carr 2005:21, 82). Over time, some of these families may have become associated with the temple or the palace (Lipiński 1988:162–4), but others probably lived far from these institutions in both geographical and social terms (Dell 2006:69–70).

Undoubtedly, the frequent references to fathers, sons and mothers in Proverbs do not necessarily suggest a family setting. In ancient Near Eastern scribal schools, teachers were called 'fathers' and students 'sons' (Carr 2005:20–1, 66–7, 82; Schipper 2019a:14). The importance of obeying mothers was also a common trope in school proverbs (for Sumerian examples, see Alster 1997:29, 170, 324), just as modern textbooks often reinforce family values. Yet family terminology most naturally reflects a family context (Goff 2020:198). Home-based training would also explain why Proverbs contains so much material which is not directly relevant to scribes. The curriculum must have been moulded by the diverse demands of a family home.

Education not only for scribes

So far, we have a straightforward story with just a few debated details. There was an Israelite scribal school or perhaps more than one. The word 'school' may be misleading, as it did not necessarily require a separate building, but, presumably, there was a centralized scribal education from at least the eighth century BCE. Collections of proverbs were created by scribes to train scribes. The scholarly debate only concerns whether this training was mainly associated with the temple, the palace or the homes of master scribes.

Perhaps everyone is right and there were schools in the temple *and* in the palace *and* in households – and possibly elsewhere (Perdue 2008:70–3; see also Carr 2005:123). However, if education happened in diverse contexts, Proverbs may have been compiled to train diverse people, not only scribes.

We know that elsewhere in the ancient Near East scribal education had two phases. First, all pupils learned rudimentary writing skills; then a select few learned the art of reading and composing long discourses. Sayings were typically used in the first phase (Schniedewind 2019:18–22). Thus, Proverbs may have served the training of people who wanted to learn elementary scribal skills for use in their occupations (Carr 2011:407). Some parts of the book may have been used by royal princes or would-be courtiers (Bryce

1979:135–62; Humphreys 1978; Millar 2020:162) and others by people in the military, commerce or various skilled trades.

Literate priests, army officers, merchants and artisans may have been called 'scribes' by their contemporaries (Carr 2005:103). But many of them would not have been involved in text production, so we modern interpreters would not consider all literate members of society as 'scribes'. Carr writes about students preparing 'for various mid- to high-level positions in their society' and the education of 'multiple elites' (Carr 2011:407). Perdue writes about 'scribes and sages' (for example, Perdue 2008:100–7). The relationship between the categories of scribes and sages is not precisely defined. Were they two distinct groups or identical? Did they overlap to some extent, or did one include the other (Blenkinsopp 1995b:9–10; Crenshaw 2019:87; Dell 2020:114; van der Toorn 2007:80)? In any case, the two categories considered in tandem potentially include people who could read and write but whose professions were not reading and writing.

That there were some literate people who were not scribes is suggested by the Bible. Numerous biblical characters are depicted as reading and writing: Moses (Exod. 17.14; 24.7), Bezalel and Oholiab (Exod. 39.30), representatives of the tribes (Josh. 18.4), Samuel (1 Sam. 10.25), Isaiah (Isa. 8.1; 28.9-13; 50.4-11). Also, verses such as Deuteronomy 4.6-8; 6.7-9; 11.18-21 and Isaiah 8.16 presuppose that everyone had access to these writings. It is unlikely that everyone could read, so others would have read to them (Young 1998a:249–50). This required the presence of a higher number of literate people than the small group of fully fledged scribes.

This has been reaffirmed by some archaeological finds. For example, the famous Siloam inscription was probably an unofficial writing, as it does not mention the king and was invisible to everyone except the builders and maintainers of the Siloam tunnel (Schmid and Schröter 2021:66; see also Sanders 2009:138–9). Also, a recent analysis of the handwriting on sixth-century *ostraca* from Arad, a military outpost, indicates that at least six different individuals wrote them, including the commander of the fortress, the person in charge of the warehouse and his assistant. It is unlikely that all these men received full scribal training (Faigenbaum-Golovin 2021; Faigenbaum-Golovin et al. 2016).

Therefore, (much of) Proverbs may have served in the training of a somewhat broader literate elite. This may explain why, unlike in other ancient Near Eastern proverb collections, scribes are never mentioned in the book and why the act of writing is mentioned only once (22.20). However, it was still a book for the literate elite which was small (Carr 2005:13, 115–16; Young 1998a, 1998b). Their privileged status, some argue, left its mark on Proverbs. The frequent mention of the king, the sophisticated expressions, the praise of affluence and the frequent discussion of gaining riches and caring for the poor reveal the elitist views of the 'sages' (see Perdue 2008:54, 100; Schipper 2019a:141). These are not the concerns of the poorest members of society.

Therefore, besides the debate over the location of the education in which Proverbs was used, its target group is also contested. It may have been the scribes or a wider literate elite. Some, however, wish to go even further and suggest a broader purpose that goes beyond formal education.

Not for formal education

The literary flourishes of chapters 1–9 or 31 may entertain readers (or audiences, if we think of oral performances, see Walton 2020). The deceptively naive simplicity of the sentence literature of chapters 10–30 hides great depths (see Introduction to the Sentence Literature in Part II). There is much there to stretch the mind and broaden the horizon. If, however, Proverbs can challenge, entertain and surprise like the best of literature, perhaps it is more like literature than a textbook (Weeks 2011:471; Goldingay 2019:50; contrast with Carr 2005:133, 293).

This does not mean that no part of Proverbs was ever used in formal education. Shakespearean dramas are taught in schools even though they were not written for that. Curriculum often comprises repurposed texts (Schniedewind 2019:38).

For everyone

Once we have taken Proverbs out of the classroom, we can put it into the hands of more people. Most proverbs are not class-specific. Both a prince and a serf should realize that 'doing wrong is like a sport to a fool, but wise conduct is pleasure to a person of understanding' (10.24). It is also questionable whether Proverbs is deaf to the concerns of the lower classes. 'A slack hand causes poverty, but the hand of the diligent enriches' (10.4) connects laziness with poverty, thereby expressing the concern of an agrarian worker rather than that of a courtier (see

Crenshaw 2019:89). When 1.10-19 warns against being involved in robbery, it addresses a typical temptation of desperate people (Crenshaw 1998a:269). Mark Sneed thinks that Proverbs' interest in the concerns and temptations of different social groups only proves that it was written for scribes, since intellectuals can 'transcend their own social locations' in their thinking (Sneed 2015a:290). However, it is equally possible that the book addresses all sorts of issues because it was written for all sorts of people.

Much of the book seems to be generally applicable. Even royal images can captivate the imagination of deprived people (just as agricultural imagery must have been suggestive to courtiers; see Weeks 2010:31–2). That 'the wise' person is contrasted with 'the fool' throughout the book also suggests that the aim is not to form a separate professional group to provide expert services to others but to form a wise character in everyone (see Carr 2011:405; Fox 2015b:70–1; Whybray 1990:133).

If the book reflects the concerns of the whole society, it may have been created by the whole society. Westermann and Golka argued that the content and often the style of sentence literature look like folk wisdom. They concluded that we should focus on the everyday lives of ordinary people when searching for the context of the sayings (Golka 1993; Westermann 1995; see also Albertz and Schmitt 2012:336–9; Dell 2006:52–6, 76; Kimilike 2008; for a critique of such views, see Fox 1996).

Even if, in their final form, the proverbs are not folk sayings, they may incorporate folk sayings and express their world view. A relatively recent insight is that writing and orality exist in symbiosis (Vayntrub 2019:85; Weeks 2010:31). Written works are influenced by the style and content of oral performance and, in turn, influence oral performance. Written texts interact with the whole society through the mediation of those who can read. As Carr explains, a literate elite could memorize a written text 'and this elite then could perform such texts (possibly still using a written copy) for a broader, illiterate populace' (Carr 2005:160; see also Sandoval 2020b:271; Walton 2020:263–70). Therefore, parts of Proverbs may have been originally created orally, turned into writing and then transformed into spoken words again. This intricate relationship between written proverbs and oral culture is well documented in the case of Benjamin Franklin's eighteenth-century popular collection of proverbs, *Poor Richard's Almanack*. Many folk proverbs (for example, 'No pain, no gain') survived because they made it into Franklin's collection and then became popular in oral discourse (Schniedewind 2019:137).

Conclusion

- Proverbs was a textbook for future scribes who lived in the temple precincts.
- No, it was used in the palace.
- No, it was used by the heads of scribal guilds for teaching at home.
- No, it was not only for training scribes but a wider elite.
- No, it was not a textbook; it functioned as literature.
- No, it was not only for the intellectual elite; it reflected popular wisdom and was written for the benefit of the whole society.

Vayntrub is appropriately cautious when she states, '[t]here exists no available data on the social or educational function of the biblical book of Proverbs (or any of its parts) during its composition or collection. … The social function of Proverbs … cannot be determined given the available evidence' (Vayntrub 2016:98). Therefore, until archaeological or other ingenious arguments shed more light on the issue, scholars can only offer guesses. These guesses are well informed by indirect evidence on the use of proverbs in other ancient Near Eastern societies, on our limited knowledge of ancient Israelite society and on the study of proverbs in general (paremiology). Nonetheless, they are guesses.

Perhaps the text of Proverbs can accommodate contradictory theories because it has many parts with different social settings and purposes (Ademiluka 2018:169; Dell 2006:15, 88–9). Some may be literature for entertainment, others instructions for a prince and yet others collections of folk proverbs. Furthermore, the original purpose of a work does not necessarily determine how it is actually used. What was intended as a textbook may end up as literature and vice versa. As Suzanna Millar notes about the sentence literature in Proverbs, '[s]cholars cannot agree on the context, addressee, or perspective of the sayings, and this, I suggest, is because they are open to a number of contexts, addressees, and perspectives' (Millar 2020:163).

Ancient Near Eastern parallels

A watershed occurred in the study of Proverbs in 1924. This was when Erman's classic study about the *Instructions of Amenemope* and Proverbs was published. Egyptologists had known about the *Instructions of Amenemope* for several decades, but the full text had only been published in the previous year (Budge 1923). Erman pointed out a large number of close parallels between *Amenemope* and Proverbs, mainly Proverbs 22.17–24.22. Later studies have refined the list of similarities, some of which are striking. See, for example, the beginning of Proverbs 22.17–24.22 (translation by Fox 2009:757):

> Give your ears, that you may hear the things that are said (*Amenemope* 3.9)
> > Incline your ear and hear my words (Prov. 22.17b)
> apply your heart to interpret them. (*Amenemope* 3.10)
> > and direct your heart to my knowledge (Prov. 22.17c)
> They will be a mooring post for your tongue. (*Amenemope* 3.16)
> > That they may all be secure on your lips (Prov. 22.18b)

The recognition of the *Amenemope* parallels came soon after the discovery of the Aramaic *Ahiqar* (Sachau 1911:147–82) and preceded many similar discoveries of ancient Near Eastern writings containing parallels to Proverbs. The Egyptian writings are usually presented as the teachings of illustrious historical figures. The most important ones, in chronological order from approximately 2500 BCE to 500 BCE, include the *Instruction of Hardjedef*, the *Instruction of Kagemni*, the *Instruction of Ptahhotep*, the *Instruction to Merikare*, the *Instruction of Amenemhet*, the *Instruction of Ani*, the *Instruction of Amenemope*, the *Instruction of Ankhsheshonq* and the *Papyrus Insinger*. The Mesopotamian material is more diverse: numerous Sumerian proverb collections; similar collections from Hattuša and Mari; Šimâ Milka ('Hear Counsel') from Hattuša, Ugarit and Emar; and writings similar to the Egyptian instructions, such as the *Instruction of Šuruppak*, *Counsels of Wisdom*, *Advice to a Prince* and *Counsels of a Pessimist*.

The oldest in the above list are the Sumerian proverb collections predating Proverbs by over a thousand years. Considering the time gap and language barrier, any direct literary dependence is unlikely. Yet there are many similarities. Like Proverbs, these Sumerian collections contain some loosely organized proverb clusters. Here is one, comprising sayings relating to the heart.

> 1.91 My girlfriend's heart is a heart made for me.
> 1.92 Who can show what my heart has conceived(?) for me(?).
> 1.93 Where my heart … Let me go to that place.
> 1.94
> 1.95 In my heart you are a human being, but in my eyes you are not a man.
> 1.96 When the heart flows over, it is lamentable. He who can keep it in his heart is a prince.

1.97 Those who get excited should not become foremen. A shepherd should not become a farmer.

1.98 What comes out from the heart of the tree is known by the heart of the tree. (Alster 1997:22–3)

Like Proverbs, Sumerian sayings urge the son to listen to his parents; they often seem secular but occasionally mention fearing the gods, and they promote humility, diligence and righteousness. Sumerian collections, just like Proverbs, contain variants of sayings, short stories or scenes that illustrate proverbial truths (rather like Prov. 24.30-34, for example) and lists similar to the numerical sayings in Proverbs (see Prov. 30.11-33).

The Egyptian instructions have often been compared to Proverbs 1–9, but some later Egyptian works, similarly to the whole book of Proverbs, contain more or less haphazard sayings preceded by longer instructions (for example, *Ankhsheshonq* and *Insinger*). The Egyptologist Miriam Lichtheim (1996:261) describes the virtues of the ideal person in these writings as 'honesty and truthfulness; justice, kindness and generosity; temperance and patience, thoughtfulness, diligence and competence; loyalty and reliability' (Lichtheim 1996:261), a list almost identical with that in Proverbs (see Anthropology in Part II). The writers of Proverbs probably borrowed some typical phrases from the Egyptian works, such as 'weighing hearts' (Prov. 21.2; 24.12), 'chambers of the belly' (Prov. 18.8; 20.27, 30; 26.22) or 'within the belly' (Prov. 22.18a, as opposed to the typical Hebrew 'within kidneys') (McLaughlin 2018:59; Shupak 1993:339).

Many have drawn the conclusion that the authors of Proverbs were a cosmopolitan group of scribes who deliberately reworked and sometimes straightforwardly copied foreign material. This seems to be reaffirmed by the biblical portrayal of Israelite wise people.

> Biblical texts themselves attest to the international character of instructional literature. They attribute wisdom to non-Israelite sages (e.g., 1 Kgs 5:10–11 [ET 4:30-31]; Psalms 88 and 89 [both 'wisdom songs' …]; Prov. 30:1; 31:1; Job), and narratives about Solomon depict the Phoenician Hiram recognizing his wisdom (1 Kgs 5:21 [ET 5:7]//2 Chr 2:11 [ET 2:12]) and show Solomon in dialogue about wisdom with the Queen of Sheba (1 Kgs 10:1–9//2 Chr 9:1–8).
>
> (Carr 2011:408)

It is better to be cautious, though, as the following personal story suggests. A few years ago, in a friendly debate, an English friend of mine interjected, 'As the famous Hungarian proverb says, "The road to hell is paved with good intentions"'. Being Hungarian, I was touched. 'How do you know this Hungarian proverb?' I asked. He smiled and explained that he simply assumed this well-known English proverb existed in other languages – he was just bluffing. I was perplexed. In my mind, the proverb was quintessentially Hungarian. I had learned it from my parents in a rural area of Hungary where no one spoke foreign languages or read foreign literature. I could hardly imagine a less internationally exposed group of people than my working-class family. And I sensed the typical Hungarian cynicism in the proverb, surely the fruit of the painful history of the nation. Learning that it was not originally Hungarian came as a shock. This little episode illustrates the difficulty. Had I, naive, uneducated Zoltán, compiled a collection of (in my judgement Hungarian) proverbs, better-educated and internationally minded readers may have concluded that I had a thorough knowledge of other European proverbs. But they would have been wrong. Similarly, we cannot be certain how familiar the authors of Proverbs were with international literature (see Nel's argument that the international feel of proverbs can be reconciled with the theory of their folk origin (Nel 1996)).

Even the parallel between *Amenemope* (ca. 1250–1100 BCE) and Proverbs 22.17–24.22 is debated. The Hebrew text uses *Amenemope* so freely that Whybray (1994c) questioned whether there was any relationship between the two works. Although most other scholars think that *Amenemope* did indeed influence Proverbs 22.17–24.22 (Emerton 2001; Fox 2009:756–61), that influence was not necessarily direct. Some maintain that the Israelite author knew the Egyptian work (Shupak 2005). Others think that the Hebrew is dependent on a (possibly non-Hebrew) work that was dependent on *Amenemope* (Fox 2009:763–5). Yet others think that the text of *Amenemope* may have been transmitted orally for hundreds of years, during which it was often misremembered or deliberately updated before it reached the authors of Proverbs 22.17–24.22, and that the Israelite scribes were no longer aware of *Amenemope* (Carr 2005:127, 408; Schniedewind 2019:126–30).

We know from Sirach 39.34 that some scribes in the second century BCE could speak foreign languages and visited foreign countries (van der Toorn 2007:53) but we do not have any direct evidence for similar training in the monarchic period (Weeks 2011:467). Consequently, it is hard to decide to what extent the many similarities between ancient Near Eastern writings and Proverbs are due to unmediated familiarity with foreign literature. These similarities may often be the results of a common stock of phrases, concepts and themes that were widespread in the ancient Near East. Nonetheless, the similarities are undeniable, which means that studying ancient Near Eastern literature can enhance our understanding of Proverbs.

Authorship

Solomon

Proverbs 22.17–24.22; 24.23-34; 30.1-33 and 31.1-31 are not attributed to Solomon (see 22.17; 24.23; 30.1; 31.1 (on the different parts of Proverbs, see 'Collection of collections' in Part II)). But the majority of the book is. Of its 915 verses, 769 (1–9; 10.1–22.16; 25.1–29.27) seem to claim Solomonic authorship (Schipper 2019a:8) and 1.1 brings the whole book under Solomon's auspices.

Post-biblical tradition, probably because of the influence of 1.1, makes the book even more Solomonic. The Septuagint eliminates all non-Solomonic subtitles (Fox 2009:1031, 1041, 1060, 1064; for the emphasis on Solomonic authorship in the Septuagint, see Aitken 2007:197; Fox 2015a:172–3). Rabbinic tradition speculated that while Solomon wrote the Song of Songs in his youth and Ecclesiastes in old age, he wrote Proverbs in his prime and Agur and Lemuel (30.1; 31.1) were just alternative names for Solomon (*Shir HaShirim Rabbah* 1:1). The famous fourteenth-century illuminated Bible by Jean de Sy illustrated the whole of Proverbs with pictures about Solomon's life (Vayntrub 2019:183). The combined effect of 1.1 and thousands of years of interpretative tradition is that even modern readers are surprised to learn that various authors are mentioned in the book.

There are scholars who think that the traditional attribution of Proverbs to Solomon has some historical value. Some tentatively raise the possibility that some parts of Proverbs go back to Solomonic times (Clifford 1999:3–4; Dell 2004:255–7, 2020), while others affirm Solomonic authorship for much of Proverbs more firmly (Carr 2011:410; Estes 1997:16–17; Waltke 2004:31–6; Waltke and De Silva 2021:6–8). Carr notes, however, that while scholars take some prophetic attributions (for example, Hosea, Isaiah and Amos) as real historical data, most are unduly sceptical about Solomonic attributions.

And how sceptical some are! Mark Sneed uses strong words in his refutation of Waltke's argument for Solomonic authorship: 'The danger of this kind of thinking is that it would lead us back to the dark ages of pre-critical scholarship!' (Sneed 2015a:302). Just fifty years ago, a different mood prevailed. Gerhard von Rad proposed influentially that in Solomon's time there was a 'Solomonic enlightenment' in the Jerusalem court. This was characterized by an interest in foreign literature and the development of the education of the intelligentsia (von Rad 1962:139, 429–31, 1966a). Von Rad believed that much of Proverbs reflects this milieu (see von Rad 1972).

One reason why such views are out of fashion is that archaeologists have not found any remains of the great kingdom of Solomon, let alone of the 'Solomonic enlightenment' (Adams 2008:64; Grabbe 2017:146–50; Weeks 1999:110–31; Whybray 1982; but see the different evaluations of the evidence in Finkelstein and Mazar 2007:107–39 and Dell's scepticism about the use of archaeological data in such debates (Dell 2020:78–81)). The attributions to Hosea, Isaiah and Amos seem rather different than the attributions to a legendary king who lived 200 years before those prophets and for whose legendary kingdom there is no extra-biblical evidence.

In addition, it was customary in the ancient Near East to attribute instructions to famous people, usually without any historical basis (Sneed 2015a:95–6). Indeed, the authorial attributions in Proverbs seem to be later additions. Proverbs 24.23 and 25.1 read 'also sayings of the wise/Solomon'. When 24.23-34 and 25–29 were independent works, they would not have had titles beginning with the word 'also', so that word (if not the whole title) must be a later editorial addition. In 10.1 the 'sayings of Solomon' does not contain the word 'also', which suggests that the previous nine chapters are not 'of Solomon' and 1.1 is another later editorial addition (Weeks 2007:40). The book bears the signs of gradual gestation, and its different parts seem to presuppose various social locations and different times of writing. For all these reasons, most scholars doubt that Solomon was the author of much or any of Proverbs (Bellis 2018:xlv–xlvi; Longman III 2006:23–6; Murphy 1998:xx; Sneed 2015a:301–2).

Pseudonymity

Therefore, most modern scholars think that the book is pseudonymous, that is, falsely attributed to Solomon. But the role and nature of pseudonymity are contested. There is agreement that pseudonymity in general strengthens the claim for the special authority of the work in question (Dell 2006:3–4; Sneed 2015a:96; van der Toorn 2007:7, 27). However, were ancient authors and editors deliberately misleading their readers? Or was fictitious authorship a customary and perfectly transparent literary tool?

Karel van der Toorn thinks that there was an element of deception in pseudonymity. Although he acknowledges that copyright infringement and plagiarism were not such grave sins in antiquity as today (2007:45–47), he thinks that readers were probably unaware that the attribution of a pseudonymous work did not convey reliable historical information (2007:33–6).

However, he makes an interesting distinction between pseudonymity and attributed authorship. Pseudonymity 'is the strategy of an author who wishes to optimize the chances of a favourable reception of his work'. Attributed authorship, on the other hand, is the work of editors who want to explain the existing authority of a work (2007:36). Seeing the Solomonic attribution in Proverbs as 'attributed authorship' may shed a more favourable light on the ancient editors; for in that case they were not seeking any unfair advantages for their work in the thriving market of wisdom instructions but were trying to explain why Proverbs was so good and prestigious.

Some scholars want to distance even pseudonymity from deception. They argue that in ancient times there was an 'expanded concept of authorship'. The authors were not only the people who actually wrote texts but symbolic figures whose spirit were somehow expressed through the texts (Childs 1979:551; van Leeuwen 1997:20). As Farmer puts it (1991:18), the attribution should be read not as 'sayings of Solomon' but as 'Solomonic sayings', representing the kind of wisdom that characterized Solomon, the patron and muse of biblical wisdom (see also Steinberg 2019:193).

Some features of the Solomonic attributions indicate to attentive readers that they should be understood loosely. Proverbs 1.2-6 speaks about the words of the wise (1.6), not the words of Solomon. His name is missing from the rest of the book, apart from the superscriptions (1.1; 10.1; 25.1). Lady Wisdom, the mother and the father are frequently mentioned as speakers, but Solomon is curiously absent. As for the Solomonic superscriptions, they never say that Solomon created the proverbs, only that they belong to him. Also, unlike in most ancient Near Eastern didactic works, the superscriptions do not describe a specific situation in which Solomon performed the proverbs and instructions. We do not learn when, on what occasion or to whom he delivered these teachings (Vayntrub 2016; see also Fox 2003:154). Solomon never speaks. We are just informed that these are, in some sense, his proverbs.

Therefore, while Proverbs is in some way attributed to Solomon, his voice is strangely muted. Fox (2000:359) thinks that this leaves the centre stage to 'primeval, universal wisdom', Lady Wisdom herself, who speaks in chapter 8 and whose voice is embodied in the whole book. This is her book! Solomon only acts as her mouthpiece. Vayntrub (2019:184) thinks that the muted attribution to Solomon promotes not Lady Wisdom but the book itself. 'Since Solomon does not speak, it is the medium of the text itself that functions as the perpetual voice. We might say that, in Proverbs, the text – not the legendary figure named in the titles – has become the speaker.' This means that in Proverbs the authority is shifted 'from a fictional moment of speech performance to the enduring presence of the text itself' (Vayntrub 2019:113).

Hindy Najman and Irene Peirano Garrison emphasize another function of pseudonymity. It serves as an interpretative framework. Writing in the name of a famous figure engages the reader's imagination and creates new dimensions of meaning (Najman and Peirano Garrison 2019; see also Childs 1979:552; Kynes Forthcoming). Eva Mroczek also thinks that authorial attribution 'was not a religious dogma that asserts the literal authorship …, but an aesthetic, poetic, and honorific act that celebrates an ancient hero and lets him inhabit new literary homes' (Mroczek 2016:51), thereby animating and dramatizing the work (Mroczek 2016:67). These observations are particularly pertinent to Proverbs. By mentioning Solomon, the reader is encouraged to interpret the book as divine wisdom (see 1 Kgs 3.12). Alternatively, the reader can ponder how the king whose downfall was caused by foreign women (1 Kgs 11–13) can give warnings against foreign women (Prov. 6–9). Did he not listen to his own advice? Or, perhaps, Rabbi Yonatan was wrong in *Shir HaShirim Rabba* 1.1 and Proverbs was not written in Solomon's prime but at the end of his life, with the hindsight gained from his unfortunate experience with women. Either way, the Solomonic attribution stimulates a special engagement with the text.

Scribes and sages

Whether the nation's proverbs were created by kings, scribes or the 'folk genius', there must have been certain people who collected the sayings in Proverbs' sub-collections. Perhaps these people also added their own proverbs here and there (Weeks 2011:471–2). Next, someone had to stitch together the proverb collections. The introductory and closing chapters may have been added by yet another group. In all these editorial steps, highly literate scribes would have done the bulk of the work. The whole process, from the birth of an individual proverb to its incorporation into the received form of the book, may have taken hundreds of years.

Therefore, searching for a single author is probably a mistake. As van der Toorn (2007:5) explains, texts before the Hellenistic era were often coproduced 'by means of a series of scribal redactions'. There were simply no authors in the modern sense (see also Walton 2020). Michael V. Fox

(2015a:8) recommends the term 'composers' instead for those engaged in the activity of selecting and modifying texts.

There has been a shift in the scholarly opinion about the identity of these scribes. In the second half of the twentieth century especially, the standard scholarly view was that Job, Ecclesiastes and Proverbs were different from other biblical books because they were the products of a unique social group, the sages, with their unique ideology and world view. This view still has supporters (for example, Penchansky 2012:11–21), but the consensus has been broken. It has been argued that such a distinct social group was unlikely within the tiny Judahite society (Dell 2006:3–17), especially since no such separate group lay behind the didactic literature in Egypt or Mesopotamia (Carr 2011:407). Of course, the small number of literati may have formed a separate social group and within that there may have been subgroups, but it is doubtful whether they held distinct ideologies (Carr 2005; Krispenz 2021; Kynes 2019a:15–18; van der Toorn 2007; Young 1998b:418; but see Epistemology in Part II for some counterarguments).

Date

The majority view on the dating of Proverbs can be summarized in the following points (see Fox 2000:48–49, 2009a:499–500; Young, Rezetko and Ehrensvärd 2008:56–8):

- It took centuries to create Proverbs.
- Most of the sentence literature (chapters 10–29) was written in monarchic times, perhaps starting in the eighth century, though some sayings may have been created and used orally before that.
- Chapters 1–9 and parts of 30–31 were written last, in the late sixth or fifth century.
- The whole book was put together either in the Persian period (c. 550 BCE–330 BCE) or at the beginning of the Hellenistic period (c. 330 BCE–37 BCE).

These claims rest on contested assumptions and observations. Of course, those who wish to challenge the consensus build on equally debated assumptions and observations. The following is a list of these with brief notes.

Developmental paradigm

Perhaps the most important assumption is that literary forms develop from simple to complex (Ryken 2016). To put it simply, the longer a text, the later it is (for a more nuanced expression and critique of the assumption, see Vayntrub 2019:19–35). It follows from this that the longer instructions in chapters 1–9 are more recent than the simple sayings in chapters 10–29. Using the same assumption, some also argue that 10.1–22.16 and 25–29 are earlier than the other sentence collections (Vayntrub 2019:76). However, the reliability of the whole developmental principle is questionable. Anthropologists have found many counter-examples in oral traditions (Vayntrub 2019:83; see also Nel 1981:139–40). Also, longer instructions have been attested among the oldest Egyptian and Mesopotamian writings, whereas, at least in Egypt, collections of shorter sayings tend to be more recent (Carr 2011:412; Schipper 2019a:24).

It is also often asserted that, just like literary forms, ideas develop. Therefore, the more complex a thought is, the later it is. Accordingly, the theological maturity of chapters 1–9 may suggest its later date (Dell 2006:19–20). But how can the complexity of an idea be measured? At least some of the thoughts in chapters 1–9 are attested in older works. On this basis Dell proposes that even if the final form of chapters 1–9 is late, it does not follow that everything in it is late (Dell 2006:28–9).

Echoes of ancient Near Eastern texts

As I have just noted, some use ancient Near Eastern parallels to challenge a simplistic developmental paradigm and the late dating of chapters 1–9. They highlight that the one-line sayings, according to the developmental paradigm, should be the oldest, though they appear fairly late in the Egyptian material (Gemser 1960:127–8; Schipper 2019a:24). Also, the parallels between 22.17–24.22 and the *Instructions of Amenemope* are used to prove the earlier dating of 22.17–24.22 compared to 10.1–22.16, even though the latter contains simpler sayings (Steinberg 2019:193; Waltke and De Silva 2021:7). However, caution is in order. There are early one-line sayings outside Egypt and late Israelite writings could easily have been influenced by late copies of early Mesopotamian and Egyptian works (Schipper 2019a:5).

Echoes of the history of thought

Even if thoughts do not always develop from simple to complex, there are ideas that are typical of certain times. Based on this, some interpreters try to identify echoes of datable concepts in Proverbs. For example, Fox suggests that Plato's 'idea' is similar to the concept of 'wisdom' in Proverbs 1–9 (Fox 2000:355–6). However, the echoes of datable concepts such as the platonic 'idea' are usually very faint in the biblical text and it is hard to be certain about them (Carr 2011:413; Fox 2000:49).

Echoes of historical events and social contexts

Scholars also try to detect echoes of datable social developments. For example, it is asserted that chapters 1–9 presuppose an urban setting, while the rest of Proverbs is more agrarian. This suggests a later date for chapters 1–9, assuming that society gradually became urbanized. However, as Dell notes, the city imagery is limited to the depictions of Lady Wisdom and Dame Folly in chapters 1–9 and there are sayings in the sentence literature that concern city life (Dell 2016).

A famous example of a datable social development is the mass divorce from non-Israelite wives recorded in Ezra 9–10 and Nehemiah 13. The polemic against the 'strange woman' in chapters 5–9 reminds many scholars of this event. This puts chapters 1–9 roughly in the same era (fifth, perhaps fourth century BCE). However, the 'strange woman' of Proverbs does not want to marry the foolish youth (Fox 2000:48) and other ancient Near Eastern texts also warn against 'alien women' (Schipper 2019a:17, 22, 23–4; but see Weeks's (2007:132) counterargument), so this might simply be a truism and not a reflection of the social context of the Persian era.

The frequent mention of the king in the sentence literature is used to affirm its monarchic origin (Carr 2011:411). However, non-monarchic societies also have stories and sayings about royalty. (Kings and queens played an important role in the stories and folk tales of my childhood, despite growing up in communist Hungary!)

Echoes of biblical texts

Detecting echoes of datable biblical texts might seem a promising approach. However, it is notoriously difficult to establish the date of biblical texts and the direction of influence between them (an often-discussed case is the possible connection between Proverbs 1–9 and Deuteronomy, for which see the discussion in Part III).

Linguistic observations

While many have suggested pre-exilic Ugaritic, early Aramean or Israelite loanwords and grammatical features in Proverbs 10–29 (Albright 1955; Fox 2009:504; Rendsburg 2016; Waltke 2004:31–6) and post-exilic linguistic features in chapters 1–9 (Yoder 2001:15–38), the linguistic data is inconclusive (Carr 2011:412; Fox 2000:48–9, 2009:504–5).

Superscriptions

Besides Solomon, Hezekiah is the only identifiable person mentioned in a superscription (25.1). Scholars usually argue that this attribution has a greater historical weight than the Solomonic ones. Schniedewind (2004:75–7) argues that Hezekiah is only mentioned in passing, which shows that the comment does not have a propaganda value and hence is historically more reliable. However, Schipper (2019a:7) observes how Hezekiah's fame grew over time, as proved by his elevation above even Josiah in the book of Chronicles. Accordingly, emphasizing a connection with Hezekiah is not necessarily a disinterested act.

Nature of editing

Texts usually change the most at both ends, as it is easier to add prologues and epilogues than to fiddle with the middle sections. Thus, it is likely that the parts at both ends of Proverbs were added last (Carr 2005:39; Keefer 2020:12–15; van der Toorn 2007:127–8, 257–8). This argument supports the standard view that chapters 1–9 and 30–31 are later additions. However, Carr notes that it is especially easy to attach new material to the end of a scroll. He argues that if we accept that Proverbs 25–29 was written in the eighth century, then it is likely that chapters 1–24 are earlier (Carr 2011:411). It is an interesting argument, but adding new material to the beginning of a scroll cannot be ruled out and it should also be remembered that newly added material may actually be older than the core of the text to which it is added.

Conclusion

None of the observations and assumptions regarding the dating of Proverbs provide certainty, which explains the dissenting voices. However, most agree it must have taken a long time to create such a diverse book (Schipper 2019a:11). This may also be true of some of its seven major parts. If the majority opinion is accepted, it suggests that the book as a whole may have been put together relatively late but contains old (pre-exilic) material. In this case it is unlikely that the unique features of Proverbs, such as its lack of interest in history, can be explained by its very early or very late date, since its creation overlapped with the creation of many other biblical books.

Selected works

Scribal culture in the ancient Near East

On literacy and scribal education in the wider ancient Near East, compare Carr (2005:3–109), Sanders (2017:3–10) and van der Toorn (2007:51–73). Zhakevich (2020) detects Egyptian influence on Israelite scribes. Schniedewind (2019) emphasizes the impact of the Mesopotamian curriculum.

Scribal culture in Judah and Israel

The best introduction to Israelite literacy, scribal education and related epigraphic data is still Rollston Rollston (2010). For alternative views and recent epigraphic finds, see Burlingame (2019), Carr (2005:111–73), Davies (1995), Dell (2020:112–28), Demsky (2014), Lemaire (2001), Na'aman (2015), Rollston (2018), Schniedewind (2019), Shmuel and Mazar (2014:63) and Young (1998a, 1998b).

Orality

For the relationship between oral culture and written artefacts, see Carr (2005), Fox (2003:160–5), Niditch (1996), Sandoval (2020b), van der Toorn (2007), Vayntrub (2019:70–102), Walton (2020), Weeks (2011:12–14) and Zinn (2018:72–8).

Folk origin

The classic works that argue for the folk origin of proverbs are Golka (1993) and Westermann (1995). Akoto-Abutiate (2014:133–41) and Lucas (2015:39–40) provide overviews of the scholarly reception of Golka's work. Kimilike (2002) develops Golka's argument.

Solomon

For the original statement of the 'Solomonic enlightenment' consult von Rad (1966a) (German edition published in 1944). The idea has been refuted by many, for example, Weeks (1999:110–31). Dell (2020) is sceptical about such a straightforward refutation. For different assessments of the archaeological evidence, see Finkelstein and Mazar (2007:107–39).

Authorship and pseudepigraphy

Van der Toorn (2007:27–49) and Walton (2020) compare our concept of an 'author' with ancient literary practices. Mroczek (2016:51–85) and Najman and Garrison (2019) point out that pseudepigraphy creates an interpretative context. Klawans (2019:1–38) explains different approaches to the relationship between pseudepigraphy and forgery.

Ancient Near Eastern parallels

See Fox (2011), Lucas (2015:29–38), Schipper (2019a:17–24) and Weeks (2007:4–32, 2010:9–22). The ancient texts can be found in Alster (1997, 2005), Hallo and Younger (2003), Lambert (1996) and Lichtheim (1973). For *Amenemope*, see Fox (2009:753–67, 2014) and Shupak (2005).

Part II
The literary context

Collection of collections

Proverbs is not one book but at least seven. It begins with the title 'The proverbs of Solomon son of David, king of Israel' but then has six further titles, apparently starting six more 'books':

10.1: 'The proverbs of Solomon'
22.17: 'The words of the wise'
24.23: 'These also are sayings of the wise'
25.1: 'These are other proverbs of Solomon that the officials of King Hezekiah of Judah copied'
30.1: 'The words of Agur son of Jakeh'
31.1: 'The words of King Lemuel'.

In all likelihood, some of these 'books' were also compiled from different sources. The titles in 22.17 and 24.23 refer to groups of authors, thereby suggesting that the sayings of several different individuals were collected. The changes in style and content within some collections also suggest that they might have had different sources. Thus, Proverbs is not simply an anthology but an anthology of anthologies.

As discussed in Part I, Proverbs 1.1 gives a Solomonic veneer to the whole work. It suggests that the book, even if authored by many people, represents Solomonic wisdom, the kind that was divinely revealed to Solomon according to 1 Kings 3. If, instead of Solomon, the reader focuses on the many-authored anthological nature of the book, it has a similarly awe-inspiring effect. It suggests that the book is a truly comprehensive work, containing all the wisdom of many generations (Vayntrub 2019:198).

I provide a guided reading of Proverbs' seven sections in Part II, besides a general introduction to sentence literature (following the discussion of Prov. 1–9) and a reflection on the unity and world view of the book (following the discussion of Prov. 31).

Chapters 1–9

The main building blocks of chapters 1–9 are the introduction and a series of speeches by a certain father, or by a father and a mother, or by an unspecified parent addressing a son or sons. These speeches are usually introduced by parental appeals to listen. They are often called 'instructions' in academic parlance, based on the model of Egyptian instruction literature, although it is questionable whether instruction was an established genre with well-defined rules (Schipper 2019a:49). There are also speeches by a personified feminine character I will call Lady Wisdom. Surprisingly, however, the very last speech (9.13-18) is given by a negative figure, Dame Folly. In addition to all these speeches, there are two sections (6.1-19 and 9.7-12) that are composed of short maxims, though it is possible to understand them as belonging to the previous speeches.

Introduction 1.1-7	Parental speeches	Wisdom's speeches	Folly's speech	Maxims
	1.8-19			
		1.20-33		
	2.1-22			
	3.1-10			
	3.11-20			
	3.21-35			
	4.1-9			
	4.10-19			
	4.20-27			
	5.1-23			
				6.1-19
	6.20-35			
	7.1-27			
		8.1-36		
		9.1-6		
			9.13-18	9.7-12

Regarding this structure, there are several debated points, most of which concern chapter 3. Despite the parental appeal in 3.11-12, which is the usual way of starting a new section (as in the table above), most scholars take 3.1-12 as one speech (for example, Fox 2000:152; van Leeuwen 1997:50–3; Schipper 2019a:135; but note the dissenting voice of Weeks 2007:48–51, 100–1). Many think that the middle speech in chapter 3 (whether it begins in 3.11 or 3.13) is not a parental speech but an interlude (Fox 2000:44–5; Schipper 2019a:57–8), although some note that it may be uttered by a parent (Loader 2014:165–6; Murphy 1998:20; Weeks 2007:100–2). If it is not, we are left with ten parental speeches (or 'instructions') supplemented by other material: the speeches of Wisdom and Folly, the maxim sections and 3.13-20. Most commentators agree that there are ten parental speeches, though some reach this number without removing 3.13-20 from the list. Waltke, for example, takes the second and third speeches in chapter 3 as one lecture (3.13-35; Waltke 2004; Waltke and De Silva 2021:97–106). Loader takes 3.1-12 and 3.13-26 as two speeches and considers 3.27-35 to be an additional poem (Loader 2014:8, 183–4).

Although the parental addresses clearly divide Proverbs 4 into three sections, some commentators think that the whole chapter can be seen as a unity (Fox 2000:176; Schipper 2019a:175–6, 178). The precise nature of 9.7-12 and its relationship to its context is also contentious (compare Byargeon 1997; Fox 2000:306–18).

Most scholars agree that the text was produced in stages, but the details are debated. Many argue that the text originally comprised some parental speeches to which additional material was added. The usual suspects for these additions are Proverbs 1–2, 3.13-20, 6.1-19 and 8–9. Correspondingly, some see multiple authors and editors behind the text (Whybray 1994b:11–61). Others think that the core of the text was written by a single author whose work was later emended (Fox 2000:322–30; Schipper 2019a:49–52). There are also scholars who think that (almost) everything was written by one person (Weeks 2007:44–51).

1.1-7

The book begins with an extraordinary promise: this book can turn its readers into receptive students (1.2), moral (1.3) and shrewd persons (1.4), good speakers and leaders (1.5) and insightful scholars (1.6), but only if they humble themselves before YHWH (1.7).

This paraphrase requires some justification. In 1.5 the word 'learning' (NRSV) refers to knowledge that is expressed in eloquent speech (see 16.23: 'the mind of the wise … adds persuasiveness to their lips', where 'persuasiveness' is the same Hebrew word). The other promised accomplishment in the same verse is 'skill' (NRSV). The Hebrew word usually refers to the skill of guiding others (see 11.14; 20.18; 24.6). As for 1.6, the things that the reader is supposed to understand (proverbs, figures, words of the wise, riddles) are playful, enigmatic forms of expression, requiring the ability to look below the surface and see what is not immediately obvious (Fox 2003:167; Millar 2020:30–5; Noegel 2021:28, 128–9; Sandoval 2007:471).

A striking feature of the introduction is its holistic nature (Goldingay 2014). It mentions attentiveness (1.2), moral character (1.3), shrewdness (1.4), managerial (1.5) and hermeneutical (1.6) skills; a list which sounds surprisingly unconnected to modern ears. In the world of the author no one can be a truly effective leader (1.5) unless they have a moral character (1.3) and can reflect upon the enigmas of the wise sayings of former generations (1.6). What is missing from this introduction is equally striking. Some of the main promises of the rest of Proverbs are riches, honour and long life (for example, 3.16; 8.18, 35; 13:14; 21.20; 22.4). None of these rewards feature here.

The prologue makes its extraordinary promise in an extraordinary style. Almost each verse in 1.2-6 has two parts (a part is called a *stich* or *colon* and the two parts together are known as a *distich* or *bicolon*) and, in the Hebrew, each *colon* has three words and starts with the letter *lamed* (meaning 'to/for'). This rhythm is broken twice: first in 1.3b, where 'righteousness, justice and equity' is not preceded by *lamed*, which may draw the reader's attention to the special importance of moral character (Brown 1996:23–30; Sandoval 2007:461) and second in 1.5, which has more words and whose *cola* do not start with *lamed*. While the previous sentences are purpose clauses that seem to depend on 1.1 ('The proverbs of Solomon … for learning … for understanding … for gaining …'), 1.5 is different.

Understanding 1.5 within its context has caused interpreters some headaches and led to a debate concerning the book's implied audience. There are four main options. First, some think that 1.5 may be a later interpolation (Clifford 1999:34; van Leeuwen 1997:32; Whybray 1994b:54). If deleted, the remaining introduction has a simple meaning: this book is written to educate inexperienced young people (see 1.4). Second, many think that there are two sentences in 1.1-6; the first in 1.1-4, describing the book's benefits for the naive young, and the second in 1.5-6, describing the benefits for the wise (Brown 2014:30–1; Schipper 2019a:9–11, 62; Yoder 2009b:4–6). Third, Sandoval (2007) has proposed that while the introduction mentions two categories, the simple and the wise, the book has a single intended audience – people who consider themselves simultaneously to be simple children longing for knowledge and wise people listening judiciously to what the book has to say. Finally, Keefer (2017) argues that 1.1 is independent from the rest and the whole of 1.2-6 depends on 1.5. His understanding could be expressed like this: 'For learning about wisdom … [and] for teaching shrewdness to the simple (1.1-4), the wise shall … gain in learning (1.5), [and that will also help them] to understand a proverb' (1.6). This would mean that the implied audience are only the wise people. Fox (2003:154) and Loader (2014:59–61), although for different reasons, also think that the primary audience are wise people.

After the opening recommendation, we would expect a conclusion highlighting the indispensable value of the book for finding wisdom. Instead, we get a cautionary punchline – simply reading the book will achieve nothing. Ultimately, the quest for wisdom depends on whether one fears YHWH (1.7a) and is humble enough to accept instruction (1.7b). Fear of YHWH is the source, or perhaps the main principle, of wisdom (the precise meaning of 'beginning' is debated; see Schwáb 2013a). The phrase 'fear of YHWH' can have different connotations in different contexts, but the idea of humble submission to God is a constant element of it (Lasater 2019; Longman III 2021; Schwáb 2022b; Weeks 2007:113).

Verse 1.7 forms an *inclusio* (a frame at the beginning and end of a literary unit) with 1.2: 'For *learning wisdom and instruction*, for understanding words of insight' … 'The fear of YHWH is the beginning of *learning, wisdom and instruction* fools despise' (1.2, 7). The middle part of 1.7 is playfully ambiguous. The verbal 'learning' of 1.2 has become a noun and one wonders if the fear of YHWH is also the beginning of wisdom and instruction and, likewise, if fools despise learning as well as wisdom and instruction.

Most interpreters take 1.1-7 as an introduction to the whole book, not only to chapters 1–9 (Fox 2003:168; Sandoval 2007:456). Its phrases echo the other headings of the book in 10.1, 22.17, 24.23, 25.1, 30.1 and 31.1 (Schipper 2019a:9). If this is so, the emphasis on the need for interpretative skills to understand the enigmas of wise sayings in 1.6 warns the reader that, while the book is very rewarding, understanding it fully will not be easy. This also functions as a warning to those who find Proverbs unrewarding. Perhaps they just lack the necessary skills to understand it.

1.8-19

If the reader wonders how ethical behaviour (1.3) can be accompanied by shrewdness (1.4), a concept that is always used positively in Proverbs, the answer is given in 1.8-19. Shrewd people, if wicked, are able to trick others because they can see the consequences of words and actions that are invisible to others. But *really* shrewd people also see the inevitable and unwanted consequences of wickedness. They see that only losers are wicked (see 22.3 = 27.12).

This is illustrated in 1.8-19 by a story about wicked people who 'lie in wait for blood' and want to 'wantonly ambush the innocent' (1.11) but do not realize that they are in fact lying 'in wait for their own blood' (1.18a) and setting an ambush 'to their own lives' (1.18b). In 1.16, which states that their 'feet run to evil and they hurry to shed blood', there is a clever *double entendre*. The word for 'evil' (*ra*) can also mean 'disaster' and the second half of the verse does not specify whose blood they hurry to shed. By now the reader suspects what the wicked cannot see, that by running to evil and bloodshed they are running to disaster and shedding their own blood.

The story claims more than the simple adage that evil deeds will catch up with their perpetrators. It also suggests that if the son follows the sinners (see 1.15), he will be like the living dead. In striking language, the sinners say in 1.12, 'Let us swallow them alive like Sheol, the blameless like those who go down to the Pit.' The phrase 'those who go down to the Pit' refers to dead or half-dead people elsewhere (see Ps. 28.1; 30.3 [H. 30.4]; 88.4 [H. 88.5]; 143.7; Isa. 38.18; Ezek. 26.20; 31.14, 16; 32.25, 29, 30). Here, the parallelism between 12a and 12b suggests that it is not a description of the victims but the self-description of the sinners (Weeks 2007:194). Therefore, as they compare their power to that of death, they unwittingly give away what they really are: zombies. (The zombie apocalypse is not a modern nightmare. Ancient Near Eastern people dreaded that the dead would return to this world and devour the living. See lines 19-20 in the *Descent of Ishtar*, CDLI 2015.)

The moral of the story is that the son, addressed in 1.8-9, should be shrewder than these stupid sinners. He should see through their scheming and recognize that following them will lead to death of his inner life and then of his body.

1.20-33

Having observed the foolishness of the invitation of the wicked (1.8-19), the son (and the reader) now hears the invitation of Wisdom herself. This is the first of Wisdom's three speeches in Proverbs 1–9 (1.20-33; 8.1-36; 9.1-6). In all three, she cries out in busy, public places and invites the 'simple' (1.20-22; 8.1-5; 9.4-5). More broadly, this is the first in a series of speeches by women. The 'strange woman' and Dame Folly also cry out in busy, public places and invite the simple (7.6-7, 11-12; 9.14-16).

A peculiar feature of Wisdom's first speech is its many similarities to the speeches of the prophets. Jeremiah 7 and 20 are especially often noted as parallels (Crenshaw 1998a:196; Harris 1995:87–109; Zabán 2012:99–109; but compare with Carr (2011:420) who is sceptical about prophetic allusions). Her speech also resembles some utterances of YHWH (Schipper 2019a:99). For example, she speaks about pouring out her spirit (1.23) or stretching out her hand (1.24; not a helping hand but an ancient Near Eastern expression of might), actions that are reminiscent of YHWH's actions elsewhere (Isa. 44.3; Ezek. 14.13).

Thus, Wisdom speaks with the authority of YHWH. But her message comes as a blow. It is much harsher than her later speeches (compare 1.28 with 8.17). She assures us that she will show no mercy if people who do not listen to her get into trouble. She will laugh at them and mock them (1.26). Her rejection challenges modern sensibilities. Goldingay even thinks that Wisdom cannot really mean what she says, just like a loving mother does not mean it when she tells her child, 'Don't come crying to me when it happens' (Goldingay 2014:14).

Wisdom's harshness grows gradually. First, she speaks to the simple, encouraging them to listen (1.22-23). Then she warns them that she will laugh in their faces if they call out to her when trouble comes because of their foolishness (1.25-27). Finally, she stops talking to them, turning instead to the general audience, describing the despicable state of the panic-stricken fools who have rejected her invitation because they hate knowledge and the fear of YHWH (1.28-31; see 1.7).

The message is not unlike that in 1.8-19: actions have consequences. It is the waywardness of the simple and the complacency of fools that destroy them (1.32). Both 1.8-19 and 1.20-33 emphasize poetic justice: people get what they give. What 1.20-33 may add to 1.8-19 is that there is a point of no return. By continuously resisting Wisdom's invitation the last chance is lost.

It is not unusual to start a biblical book with divine harshness. Harris, for example, has drawn attention to Psalm 2, where God laughs at the nations (Harris 2000). But Proverbs 1.20-33 is one of the harshest beginnings in the Bible. It really 'puts the fear of God' into readers. It is imperative to adhere to the book's admonitions while they can.

2.1-22

After hearing the extravagant recommendation of the book (1.1-7), the passionate warning about following sinners (1.8-19) and Wisdom's harsh speech (1.20-33), we hear a more measured voice. The statements are no less extraordinary. Among other things, the chapter promises wisdom, knowledge, understanding and fear of God (2.5-6), the characteristics of the ideal king in Isaiah 11.2 (Schipper 2021:151–2). However, the chapter makes these promises not in the staccato clauses of 1.1-7 or the crying imperatives of 1.8-33, but in a breathtakingly complex conditional sentence – possibly the longest Hebrew sentence in the Bible. Its structure is as follows:

1-4: Seek wisdom because if you do,	(four verses)
5-8: You will understand the fear of YHWH,	
because YHWH gives wisdom,	(four verses)
9-11: You will also understand moral life,	
because wisdom comes into your heart,	(three verses)
12-15: In order to save you from the ways of evil people,	(four verses)
16-19: And to save you from the ways of the 'strange woman,'	(four verses)
20-22: So that you will not be cut off from the land.	(three verses)

The sentence has two halves (1-11; 12-22), each divided into three strophes of matching length (4-4-3; 4-4-3 *bicola* in each half). In Hebrew, each of the first three strophes begins with the letter *aleph* (disregarding the address 'my son' in 2.1), the first letter of the alphabet, while the remaining three strophes begin with *lamed*, the first letter of the second half of the alphabet. The first half focuses on what will be gained by the son: the fear of YHWH, moral character and wisdom. The second half explains how these will protect against evil people, strange women and deportation.

The chapter is like a table of contents (Koptak 2003; Schipper 2019a:121, 2021:1; Wilson 2017) that lists the key topics of chapters 1–9. For instance, the first three verses of Proverbs 2 are almost exact quotations of 7.1, 5.1 and 8.1 (Heim 2013:78–93). The promises to defend against evil people (2.12-15) and the 'strange woman' (2.16-19) capture the main concerns of the two halves of Proverbs 1–9; chapters 1–4 mainly focus on evil people and chapters 5–9 on women. Chapter 2 also picks up the main concerns of 1.1-7: the beginnings of the second and third strophes with their emphasis on the fear of YHWH (2.5) and 'righteousness, justice and equity' (2.9) echo 1.7 and 1.3b, the two focal points of the introduction.

It is often noted that in chapter 2 wisdom provides the fear of YHWH and not vice versa as in 1.7. Several interpretations have been offered. (1) A few scholars argue that it is possible to understand all verses in Proverbs 1–9 as teaching that wisdom generates the fear of YHWH (Weeks 2007:113–19; O'Kelly 2022). (2) Some take the apparent contradiction to represent two rival visions of the relationship between wisdom and piety

(Schipper 2019a:38, 109, 2021:166–7). (3) Some resolve it by saying that the sapiential quest starts with the fear of YHWH, leads to wisdom and ends in an even greater fear of YHWH (Fox 2000:111; O'Dowd 2017). (4) Others reconcile these verses by emphasizing that neither 1.7 nor 2.5-8 describes a temporal order and both envisage the fear of YHWH as an essential part of wisdom (Schwáb 2013a; 2013c:133–5).

A major theological issue addressed by the complexities of the chapter is the relationship between human and divine action. The first four verses suggest that the success of the wisdom quest depends on human action: one must accept (2.1), listen (2.2), cry out (2.3) and seek (2.4) in order to become wise. But then 2.5-8 informs us that everything depends on God because wisdom comes from him. The development of moral character (2.9-11) is usually taken to depend grammatically on 2.1-4, but it can also be dependent on 2.5-8 (compare Schipper (2021:76–80), who emphasizes the cooperation between human and divine actors, with Perdue (2000:89–90); and van Leeuwen (1997:45) who focuses on the divine).

Therefore, the son must do everything he can to gain wisdom, but he cannot boast about his wisdom as its real source is outside him (2.6, 10). He is a beggar who can only receive it from YHWH.

3.1-10

In Proverbs 3 we are back to the realm of imperatives. But the discussion of the theological themes of chapter 2 continues. It begins by highlighting the human responsibility to adhere to the teaching (3.1). Such adherence ensures a blessed life. Long and abundant life (3.2) and favour in the sight of God and people (3.4) are typical promises of ancient Near Eastern blessings (Fox 2000:147–8; Schipper 2019a:130). But then, just like 2.5-22, 3.5-10 claims that everything depends on YHWH. Instead of trusting and honouring one's own wisdom and wealth (3.5b; 7a; 9b), one should trust (3.5a), fear (3.7b) and honour YHWH (3.9a) because progress in life (3.6b), physical health (3.8) and affluence (3.10) depend on him.

While the theological message is clear, at the exegetical level interpreters struggle with many issues. For example, to what extent should teaching (*torah*) and commandments (*mitswot*) be identified with the law (compare Fox 2000:142–3; Schipper 2019a:126–7)? Does the phrase 'faithfulness and loyalty' (3.3) refer to divine or human faithfulness and loyalty (compare Fox 2000:144–5; Waltke 2004:241)?

3.11-20

By now the reader may be expecting further extravagant promises and 3.11-20 does not disappoint. It describes how wisdom provides perfect happiness, satisfying all material (3.14-16) and non-material (3.16-17) desires. This is underlined by the references to happiness at both ends of the description of wisdom's benefits (3.13, 18; for the meaning and significance of the word 'happy', see Fox 2000:161). This description follows an encouragement to accept YHWH's reproof (3.11-12) and is followed by an account of how YHWH himself used wisdom (3.19-20). Therefore, the praise of wisdom (3.13-18) is sandwiched between descriptions of YHWH's actions.

Thus, just like 1.20-33, 8.1-36 or 9.1-6, most of 3.11-20 is a poem about wisdom. However, while Wisdom speaks in those passages, here wisdom is not personified. Nonetheless, the thematic and verbal parallels, especially with chapter 8, are unmistakable. The differences, however, interest some scholars more. It is debated whether the different levels of personification and depictions of YHWH's relationship with wisdom are important. Some think that these differences may reflect different ideologies and redactional layers (contrast Fox 2000:326–9; Schipper 2019a:139–41, 147; Weeks 2007:122–3).

Proverbs 3.19-20 is especially noteworthy. Here YHWH is described as using wisdom, understanding and knowledge to create the world. The same three attributes are promised to the son in 2.6. Proverbs 24.3-4 also mentions the same triad as the tools with which one can build a luxurious house. (Bezalel and Hiram used the same tools to build the Tabernacle and the Temple respectively; see Exod. 31.1-3; 1 Kgs 7.14; van Leeuwen 2007.) There could hardly be a stronger recommendation of wisdom. It is the superpower that God used to build the universe and that we, humble human beings, can also use to build our own lives.

3.21-35

In 3.21-25 a reciprocal relationship is described: guard competence ('sound wisdom' NRSV) and prudence and they will guard you. If you do so, your confidence can be placed (and here comes the surprise) not in your competence and prudence that guard you, but rather 'YHWH will be your confidence and will keep your foot from being caught' (3.26). The second half of the section (3.27-35) has a similar pattern. It addresses the human level first (do not act unethically towards others) and then reveals the divine level (unethical behaviour is an abomination to YHWH). While 3.21-26 promises the son that he will not be harmed, 3.27-35 orders him not to harm others. In both cases, the ultimate explanation is God: do not be afraid because YHWH is your confidence; do not harm others because YHWH is their defender.

The section stresses two equations that underlie the whole of Proverbs 1–9: wisdom is a relationship with YHWH and wisdom is moral life. In this world, intellectual insight, moral action and devotion to YHWH are interrelated.

The frequency of negative admonitions in 3.27-31 is striking: 'Do not withhold good,' 'Do not say to your neighbour,' 'Do not plan harm,' 'Do not quarrel' and 'Do not envy'. These are similar to Israelite laws (see the Ten Commandments) which suggest that wisdom advice and legal commandments are not that far from each other (see Blenkinsopp 1995b; Gerstenberger 1965:49–51; Kynes 2019b:39–40; O'Dowd 2009; Schipper 2019a:164, 2019b; see also the recent trend of perceiving ancient Near Eastern laws as non-legislative moral teachings, not unlike sapiential admonitions; Fitzpatrick-McKinley 1999; Walton 2020:269). Such negative admonitions are prevalent throughout chapters 3–4. 'Do not' appears here with the highest frequency in the entire Hebrew Bible. The exception is 3.13-20 where there is not a single negative admonition, another indication of its different nature (see the discussion in the introduction to 1–9).

4.1-9

The previous chapters highlighted the dialectic relationship between human effort and the divine gift: do everything you can to obtain wisdom but accept it as YHWH's gift (1.1-7; 2.1-5; 3.1-10). Most of the punchlines and key verses were about YHWH's role. In 4.1-9 (and the rest of the chapter), the emphasis is on the human side. YHWH is not even mentioned. Wisdom, in 4.1-4, comes from human tradition: 'I teach you, my boy, what I was also taught by my father.' When 4.5-9 describes the content of that (grand) fatherly teaching, its main point is the importance of human effort: 'Get wisdom – that is the secret of becoming wise.' However, this is hardly a denial of YHWH's role. By now it is obvious that the parental teaching is a channel for God's teaching and listening to the father is an expression of the fear of God (see Fox 2000:178).

This section also picks up the theme of the reciprocal relationship between wisdom and human beings. If the son is willing to keep and guard wisdom, he will be kept and guarded by her (compare 4.4, 6 with 1.25-27; 3.21, 25-26, 34).

The imagery of 4.6-9 gives us a clue about how wisdom defends us against temptations. Wisdom is described here similarly to personified Lady Wisdom in 1.20-33, 8.1-36 and 9.1-6. The son is supposed to 'love her' (4.6b) and 'embrace her' (4.8b) and in exchange 'she will place' on his head 'a fair garland' and 'a beautiful crown' (4.9). This seems to associate parental teaching with erotic passion. It is not enough to accept the father's teaching. The son must love it as passionately as loving his bride – and this is how teaching defends him against temptation. He can resist the seductive charms of the strange woman of chapters 5–9 by loving another woman, Lady Wisdom (see Aletti 1977; Boström 1990:156–7). However, not everyone sees eroticism here. Fox argues that wisdom is not a lover but a 'powerful patroness' in these verses (Fox 2000:174, 178).

4.10-19

Now the father turns from the imagery of women to the imagery of the path. The path imagery is not a new one (1.15; 2.8-9, 13, 15, 19-20; 3.6, 17, 23, 26), even if my comments have neglected it so far. Fox even calls it the 'ground metaphor' of chapters 1–9 that unifies and organizes all the other images (Fox 2000:128–9). The most emphatic use of the metaphor, however, is found here.

It is unclear if chapters 1–9 speak of two ways or many. Plural and singular nouns alternate. Even within a single verse, 4.11, both plural and singular can be found: 'In a *way* of wisdom I teach you; I lead you in *paths* of uprightness' (see also 2.8-9, 18-19). Habel famously argued for a strong contrast between the two ways. Fox thinks that chapters 1–9 use two forms of the metaphor, depending on whether it reflects various individual courses of life 'criss-crossing the landscape' or the two main directions towards life and death. Weeks argues that there is an emphasis on the plurality of possible lives, even if those can be classified into two types (Fox 2000:128–31; Habel 1972:135–9; Weeks 2007:73–7).

The debate over the number of ways is more than a nit-picking dispute on grammatical minutiae. The possibility of having more than two ways makes the image even more suggestive. First, it means that there are many ways of being good or bad. This, in turn, means that temptations are manifold. Life does not depend on one big decision to reject one bad way. Such decisions have to be made on a daily basis. Each step in life can be straight or crooked, so each has to be considered carefully (see how Chapman (2000:154–5) compares the big decision of the prophetic tradition with the myriad decisions of wisdom literature). This is best expressed at the end of the next speech, which picks up the path imagery (4.25-26). But the same idea is behind 4.14-15, which kind of says that the son must turn away from turning away (see Weeks 2007:76).

A path does not always reflect the nature of the destination. Picturesque paths can lead to ugly places (5.6). In 4.10-19, however, through a beautiful combination of the images of the way and light (4.18-19), the father promises that the good way will also be enjoyable. This may not be obvious at the beginning, but as the son walks 'the path of the righteous' (4.18), it will gradually become brighter in the light of the rising sun. Therefore, even though the imagery is different from the previous section (ways versus women), the sentiment is the same. In 4.1-9, recognizing the attractiveness 'the right woman' (wisdom) defends against bad women; in 4.10-19 recognizing the attractiveness of the right way helps to turn away from other paths.

As always, the speech contains translation challenges. One of these may have theological significance. In 4.13 the grammatically masculine 'instruction' (*musar*) is referred to using the feminine pronoun 'her'. This may suggest the identification of the father's instruction with the female figure of Wisdom (Fox 2000:180).

4.20-27

The main emphasis throughout chapter 4 is getting, keeping and guarding the father's instruction (4.1-9, 10, 13). Here it is connected with an emphasis on guarding one's inner life and behaviour. This is expressed by a list of body parts: the ear (4.20), eyes and heart (4.21), flesh (4.22), heart (4.23), mouth and lips (4.24), eyes and eyelids (4.25) and foot (4.26-27). The key is guarding the heart (4.23). While in contemporary symbolic language the heart represents the emotions, its meaning is different in the Bible. It symbolizes human orientation, including emotion and cognition often hidden from outside observer (see Janowski 2013:155–62). The heart has a reciprocal relationship with the organs of ears, eyes, lips and feet. What we hear, see and say and where we go influence our hearts (that is, our thoughts and emotions). However, ultimately, our hearts determine what we listen to, see and say and where we go.

5.1-23

Chapter 5 mentions the same body parts as chapter 4 (the ear: 5.1, 13; eye: 5.21; heart: 5.12; flesh: 5.11; mouth: 5.7; lips: 5.2-3 and foot: 5.5). It also emphasizes the importance of holding on to the father's instruction (5.1-2, 7, 23) and uses the imagery of paths (5.5-6, 8). Proverbs 5.1 is almost identical to 4.20. The chapter looks like a practical example for the theoretical teaching of Proverbs 4 (Schipper 2019a:187, 194).

It also echoes other chapters. Proverbs 5.22, just like 1.8-19 and 31-32, states that the wicked are responsible for their own demise. Proverbs 5.21, just like 3.5-10, hints at YHWH's decisive role in life. Proverbs 5.9-10 describes how the foolish son will lose his honour, life and riches, the things offered by wisdom in 3.16 (albeit using slightly different terminology). Thus, chapter 5 is a practical outworking of all preceding chapters.

The father warns the son about a certain strange woman, whom we met in 2.16-19 and will meet often later (6.20-35; 7; 9.13-18; see also 22.14; 23.27), although not all these sections are necessarily about the same woman. Her identity is hotly debated by scholars. Is she a woman outside the son's marriage bond, a woman unfaithful to her husband, a prostitute, a foreigner, someone outside the narrowly defined community of 'true Israelites', a devotee of other gods, a poetic symbol for alien cultural influences, or a symbol of foolishness? (A good introduction to this question is found in Weeks (2007:84–90, 128–47), though it contains some contested statements.) At any rate, she is a woman who talks dangerously persuasively (5.3-4).

Proverbs 5.6 states that the son (or, possibly, the woman herself) does not know where his path leads. But the father knows and he is happy to enlighten the son. As he explains, the son will first give his honour, life and wealth to strangers, presumably to the community of the strange woman (5.7-10). Then, at the end of his life, he will realize what a fool he has been to hate his father's instruction. He will be devastated and lonely (5.11-14). Fortunately, the father also reveals how the son can avoid such a fate. Using erotic imagery reminiscent of the Song of Songs (compare 5.3 with Song 4.11, 5.15 with Song 4.15 and 5.19 with Song 2.7; 3.19), he urges him to be intoxicated by the love of his own wife (see 4.6-9).

In this chapter, wisdom-instruction (5.1-2), sex (5.18-20), belonging to a community (5.14) and YHWH (5.21) are related. But details are unclear and it is difficult to differentiate between metaphor and literalness. This is why the chapter is so powerful. Historians searching for indisputable clues to the author's social setting may be frustrated, but poets who revel in suggestive imagery will love it (see, for example, the evocative image 'caught in the ropes of their sin'; 5.22b).

6.1-19

This section interrupts the series of teachings about the strange woman. It comprises four sayings. The first two discuss foolish people who harm themselves and then give advice about how to avoid the damage. The last two discuss evil people who harm others, but no advice is given, perhaps because they are hopeless.

Saying I (6.1-5) is about people who risk impoverishment through carelessly vouching for others. Saying II (6.6-11) is about laziness that leads to poverty. Saying III (6.12-15) is about villains who sow discord. Saying IV (6.16-19) lists different kinds of evil people. In numerical sayings, the often unexpected main point comes at the end. In this case, 6.16-18 lists obvious forms of wickedness, but the punchline mentions the pinnacle of wickedness: those who sow discord, the very topic of saying III. Sayings III and IV use similar vocabulary and concepts: the evil man (6.12, 18), misleading speech (6.12, 17), the eye (6.13, 17), feet (6.13, 18), fingers and hands (6.13, 17), heart (6.14, 18), devising (6.14, 18) and discord (6.14, 19).

It is not entirely clear why 6.1-19 is inserted here. Perhaps its function is to foreshadow the second half of Proverbs, thereby connecting chapters 1–9 to the rest of the book. The style and topics of 6.1-19 are very similar to the sentence literature of chapters 10–30. It even contains many quotations from that part of Proverbs (6.8 = 30.25b; 6.10-11 = 24.33-34; 6.13 = 16.30; 6.14 = 16.28a (see also 10.10); 6.15a = 24.22a; 6.15b = 29.1b; 6.19a = 14.5b).

Weeks (2007:224–5, 2010:42–3) thinks that an editor may have wanted to break up the prurient discussion of the 'strange woman' in chapters 5–7, and the reason for inserting the section here may simply be the arbitrary presence of the catchword 'caught' (5.22; 6.2). However, 6.1-19 has more connections with the previous chapter. In 6.1 the key word of chapter 5, 'stranger', is repeated (see 5.10, 17, 20). Most of the body parts listed in chapter 5 are repeated in 6.12-15 and in 6.16-19. While 5.21 informed us that YHWH observes the lives of people, 6.15-19 reveals the criteria he uses. All these link 6.1-19 with the discussion of the strange woman in chapter 5 (but see the contrasting view of Fox 2000:226). The discussion of the different evil people in 6.1-19 also echoes the sinners and evildoers of 1.8-19 and 2.15-18. Thus, the purpose of 6.1-9 may be to connect the two villains of chapters 1–9, the strange woman and evildoers (similarly Plöger 1983:108). Perhaps the message is that the nature and temptation of evildoers and the strange woman are not very different.

6.20-35

Following the interlude of 6.1-19, we are back to parental instructions. This one starts with the usual message: keep the instructions (6.20) and they will keep you (6.22, 24; compare 1.25-27; 3.21, 25-26, 34; 4.4, 6; 5.1-2, 7-8). As in chapter 5, they will keep the son from the strange woman (6.24), whose first-mentioned weapon is her speech (6.24b; compare 5.3-4), although her beauty is also appealing (6.25). What is different here is the active role of her husband (6.26, 29, 34-35).

Fox (2000:237) summarizes the message memorably: 'Keep away from a man's wife, or he'll beat the hell out of you,' though not all the subtleties of the passage are captured by this compact summary. The father uses two comparisons. First, he compares the adulterer to someone visiting a prostitute (6.26) and notes that while a prostitute is only after her client's money, a married woman threatens his life. Second, he compares the adulterer to a thief. A hungry thief's crime may be understandable, but he must pay for the stolen food if caught. However, while a thief loses materially, an adulterer loses his life (6.32). Perhaps this second example is not a comparison but an identification in which the thief is a poetic image of the adulterer. If so, the father acknowledges the almost irresistible power of the sex drive ('Thieves are not despised who steal only to satisfy their appetite' 6.30) but highlights that however understandable their motivation, thieves/adulterers will be punished (Schipper 2019a:248).

Between the two comparisons the father uses two proverbs: 'Can a man hold fire in his bosom without his clothes getting burned? Can a man walk on glowing embers without his feet being scorched?' (6.27-28). These proverbs play on the similarity of the Hebrew words *ishah* (woman/wife), *ish* (man) and *esh* (fire). Holding the wife of another man (*eshet ish*, 6.26) in your heart will burn you as surely as holding fire in your bosom (Perry 2008:165–6).

It is striking that in this speech (and throughout Proverbs) the father thinks his rational teaching can defend the son from erotic passion. The power of desire is noted but it is assumed that it can be controlled by reason (Fox 2009:934–45; Schipper 2019a:242, 251). Alternatively, the strange woman is a symbol for false teaching, in which case right teaching counters false teaching rather than erotic passion (see Weeks 2007; contrast with Forti 2007, 2020:181).

7.1-27

Chapter 7 begins by stating again that the son should keep the parent's teaching in order to be kept by it (7.1-5; see 1.25-27; 2.1-4; 4.4, 6; 3.21, 25-26, 34; 5.1-2, 7-8, 16; 6.23-24). In particular, he will be kept from the strange woman (7.5). In 7.4 there is the hint of a suggestion that he can get married to the parental teaching as if it were a woman (see Waltke 2004:369–70; Waltke and De Silva 2021:144; Loader 2014:297–9; Forti 2020:185–6). If this interpretation is right (for hesitancy about it, see Fox 2000:240–1), it is a striking personification (see also my comments on 4.1-9).

We are invited to look through the teacher's window (7.6) and observe a simple-minded fellow (7.7) who is wandering dangerously close to the house of the strange woman (7.8-9). She approaches him (7.10) and we hear her speak to the silent, passive boy. Just like the teacher (7.2), she too has a 'teaching' (7.21; on the basis of this parallel, Bellis (1996) speculates that the teacher may be female). Again, the idea is familiar: the main weapon of the strange woman is her smooth talk (see 2.16; 5.3; 6.24).

Her initial words sound innocent. She has slaughtered some animals for well-being offerings, so she needs help to consume them quickly (see Lev. 7.16). But her behaviour is immodest, her language is replete with sensual images familiar from the Song of Songs (Arbel 1995; Imray 2013) and her message gradually becomes explicit. At the end, it is the simple boy who is 'slaughtered' (7.22-23; for translation and interpretation, see Fox 2015a:146–48; Loader 2014:312–14; Schipper 2019a:274–76).

We have seen these motifs before in connection with the strange woman (chapters 2 and 5-6) and with the evildoers (chapters 1-4). Compare, for example, the path in 7.8 with 5.8; the darkness in 7.9 with 4.18-19; the body parts in 7.3, 7, 10-11 with 4.20-27; the invitation to simple boys in 7.18 with 1.11; lying in wait in 7.12 with 1.11, 18; setting up traps in 7.22-23 with 1.17; restless feet in 7.11 with 1.16; and Sheol in 7.27 with 1.12. Thus, chapter 7 provides little new information. What it adds is a memorable story in vivid language. In 7.10, for example, the teacher says literally, 'Look – a woman – toward him – prostitute's garb – determined heart' (for the difficulty of translating the last phrase, see Kozlova (2021); Schipper (2019a:266)), as if the teacher is whispering under his breath what he can see through the window. At last, we see the strange woman in action. And it is so difficult to resist her charms!

8:1-36

The strange woman has occupied the stage for a long time. Now Lady Wisdom enters in full glory. In 8.1-11 we hear the good news of Proverbs: Wisdom speaks loudly (8.1), publicly (8.2-3), to everyone including fools (8.4-5), and says noble, honest, true, reliable things (8.6-9) and her message dispenses more than we can imagine (10-11).

In the second part of the speech (8.12-21) Wisdom explains how she provides leaders with what they need (compare 8.12-13 with 1.4, 7 and 2.5-6). She promises the qualities of the salvific king of Isaiah 11.2 (8.13-14; see 2.5-6). She enables good government (8.15-16) and gives wealth, righteousness, justice and other things that a successful ruler needs (8.17-21).

The third part (8.22-31) explains why she is such an expert regarding leadership. She has been with God since the beginning of creation. She can teach rulers how to 'engrave' (*haqaq*) decrees (8.15) as she saw God engraving (*haqaq*) the horizon on the face of the deep (8.27) and the foundations of the earth (8.29).

In the concluding part (8.32-36) she urges her audience to listen to the instruction and to love her in order to live and be happy.

This is the most discussed chapter in the book, so it is impossible to cover everything here. But two issues deserve mention. The first is the relationship between Lady Wisdom and YHWH. Scholars debate whether she is a creature, an aspect, a hypostasis, a helper, a mediator or a child of God (Fox 2000:352-7; Lenzi 2006; Schroer 2000:18-30; Schwáb 2013c:177-87). Confusingly, she speaks with divine authority, but she is clearly not YHWH (for the significance of this issue for post-biblical Christology and kabbalistic (Jewish mystical) interpretation, see Loader 2014:367-75). Many suspect that her portrayal may have been modelled on an ancient Near Eastern goddess, though it is debated which one is meant and whether this should influence our interpretation at all (Bledsoe 2013:121, n. 5; Schweitzer 2012; Sinnott 2005). Several translational enigmas are related to this first issue. Should *qanani* in 8.22 be translated as 'created me', 'begot me' or 'acquired me' (Baumann 1996:116-18; van Leeuwen 1997:92; Schipper 2019a:3-8; Venter 2016:7)? Should *amon* in 8.30 be translated as 'master worker', 'child' or 'continually' (Schipper 2019a:312-13; Venter 2016:7-8; Weeks 2006)?

The second issue is not contested; it is simply striking. Lady Wisdom is not a long-faced, tedious, boring teacher but a boisterous woman who shouts merrily (8.3; for this connotation of 'cry out', see Schipper 2019a:296); she is a delight (of God? – see 8.30); she rejoices in God's creation and delights in humanity (8.31). She loves and should be loved passionately (8.17, 21, 36). The message is unmistakable. Searching for wisdom and living with her is not a dreary grind but a pursuit full of singing, love, joy, happiness, play and delight (see Fox 2000:294). Yet finding her is a matter of life or death (8.32-36).

9.1-18

In the grand finale of chapters 1–9 two female figures compete. The first, Lady Wisdom (9.1-6), who encouraged her audience at the end of chapter 8 to wait eagerly at her doors (8.34), prepares her house for a great feast (9.1-2). The other, Dame Folly (9.13-18), is suspiciously similar to the strange woman of chapters 5–7; she is loud (9.13; 7.11), her house is associated with Sheol (9.18; 7.27) and she offers stolen water (9.17; 5.15; for further similarities, see Schipper 2019a:323; Weeks 2007:71–3), although it is contested whether the strange woman and Dame Folly are identical (contrast Forti 2007; Fox 2000:262; Goff 2015; Loader 2014:397; with Blenkinsopp 1991; Yee 1989; Bellis 2018:2–3).

Lady Wisdom and Dame Folly offer similar invitations to the simple (9.4, 16) from their similarly elevated houses (9.3b, 14b). But below the surface they are different. Lady Wisdom is preparing a luxurious meal of meat and mixed (or 'spicy'? see Schipper 2019a:327–8) wine (9.2). Dame Folly is sitting idly, using clever marketing to sell her despicable stolen water and hidden bread (9.17; compare 20.17).

Lady Wisdom's seven-pillared house (9.1) may represent the book of Proverbs with its seven headings (for different interpretations of the seven pillars, see Loader 2014:382–4; Schipper 2019a:322; Schwáb 2013c:198–202; see also how Loader (2014:391) combines the house = book and house = universe interpretations). The reader is invited to enter this house, that is, the book of Proverbs, rather than Dame Folly's deadly house of false teachings.

But the six verses (9.7-12) between the descriptions of the two women (each six verses long) suggest that the book is not for everyone. These verses contrast the God-fearing wise with those who scoff at wisdom and suggest that the scoffers are hopeless (for the thematic unity or the lack thereof in these verses, see Byargeon 1997; Fox 2000:306–18; Loader 2014:380–1; Schipper 2019a:320–1). So, dear reader, if you think that the teaching in Proverbs is ridiculous and you are above it, well – do not waste your time on the rest of the book.

Introduction to the sentence literature

'Proverbs are like butterflies; some are caught, others fly away,' says a proverb. As we reach chapter 10, it feels as though hundreds of butterflies are suddenly fluttering into the air. It may be a beautiful sight, but what are we to do with them? Biblical scholars are not used to catching butterflies, certainly not in these quantities. They usually hunt bigger beasts such as stories, songs, letters and legal codes. Therefore, before I continue commenting on the text, it is worth looking at some scholarly debates about what can be done with these unruly butterflies.

What is a proverb?

The Hebrew word that is often translated as 'proverb' is *mashal* (1.1; 10.1; 25.1). Its precise meaning has been debated for centuries. Herder and Gunkel took it to refer to the 'pithy pre-poetic expressions' of the common people (Vayntrub 2019:20–1). Eissfeldt (1913) and then Hermisson (1968), however, distanced *mashal* from folk proverbs. As they explained, folk proverbs tend to be simple, one-line statements ('Absence makes the heart grow fonder') whereas the sayings of Proverbs usually have two 'limbs' ('Hatred stirs up strife, but love covers all offences' (10.12)).

Mashal can also imply longer discourses (in Ezek. 17.2, the word apparently refers to the whole of 17.3-10; see also Num. 24.3, 15; Ps. 78.2; Isa. 14.4). Some, based on the word's etymology (from either 'to be like' or 'to rule'), think that it refers to all sorts of comparative or authoritative discourses, whether proverbs, longer similes or allegories (Millar 2020:32). Weeks (2010:26) skips over speculations about the meaning of the word by suggesting that it may have been chosen simply because it alliterates with the name of Solomon in Hebrew ('proverbs of Solomon' – *mishley shlomoh*). In this book I use the word 'proverb' or (following the advice of Crenshaw 1998b:67) 'saying'.

Mark Sneed thinks that it is a mistake to call the sayings 'proverbs'. Because they are not popular one-liners known to everyone, and because they are presented as belonging to Solomon, they are more like maxims or aphorisms by an author (Sneed 2015a:189). However, strictly speaking, Proverbs' presentation allows that Solomon only collected and affirmed folk sayings. Also, Proverbs does contain some one-liners (for example, 26.13-15) and two-limb folk proverbs also exist (Dell 2006:57; Vayntrub 2019:83). The borderline between proverbs and maxims is not sharply defined. Authors may copy the style and content of folk sayings (Weeks 2011:471–2) and folk sayings may be influenced by maxims (for the complexities of form-critical analysis of the sayings, see Fontaine 1982:2–27; Vayntrub 2019:76). Therefore, I will not restrain from calling the sayings 'proverbs'.

Whether *mashal* has a precise meaning or it is a vague category, whether it describes only the short sayings of Proverbs or includes its longer sections, or whether it refers to folk sayings or artistic aphorisms, the characteristics of Proverbs' short sayings are clear. Most consist of two statements written in a terse style. Ellen F. Davis claims that each proverb is a tiny poem (Davis 2019:337). She has a point; just like the best poems, a proverb can only be fully appreciated if the reader takes time to meditate on it.

Boring or thought-provoking?

Proverbs 1.1-7 promises that Solomon's proverbs will benefit us greatly, but the first nine chapters contain few proverbs. Instead, the father and Lady Wisdom promise that their teaching will provide life, riches and honour, but again, they give little guidance beyond encouraging us to listen to their guidance. In chapter 9 we read that Lady Wisdom is preparing a luxurious meal and our appetites are whetted for that wonderful intellectual food (see Brown 2004:137–8). But where is it?!

At last, 10.1 announces Solomon's proverbs. But many find these proverbs disappointing. They are not exactly ground-breaking. On the contrary, they often sound rather obvious ('He who gathers in summer is an intelligent son, but he who sleeps in harvest is a shameful son' (10.5)). Stuart Weeks expresses this vividly in connection with 10.1–22.16:

> Much of the first collection is characterized by advice so general that it is almost worthless: saying after saying spells out the virtues and rewards of the righteous, the wise, and the upright, along with the corresponding vices … of their counterparts. … Pretty much anyone could applaud these sayings

without in the least being motivated to change their behaviour, let alone being taught how to do so.

(Weeks 2010:32)

The sayings are also criticized for embodying a black-and-white view of people and consisting of boring mechanical repetitions (Millar (2020:11, 58, 90–1) reviews such disparaging evaluations).

Hatton (2008) disagrees. He argues that the book is full of tensions. For example, 10.3 claims that YHWH thwarts the desire of the wicked and then 10.4 says that diligence enriches. What about wicked, diligent people? Is this an oxymoron? Will they become rich (10.4) or will their cravings be thwarted (10.3)? Can both happen at the same time? Hatton highlights many such examples and it is easy to add to his list. For example, while 10.4 says that diligence makes one rich, 10.22 claims that YHWH makes one rich. Let others praise you, says 27.2, while 27.21 warns that the praise of others is a terrible trial. The righteous are as bold as a lion (28.1) but happy is the man who is never without fear (28.14). The network of (apparent) contradictions makes perceptive readers reflect on the paradoxes of life and theology. They learn either how to resolve them or how to live with them (see Gladson 1979; Hatton 2008; O'Dowd 2009:130–5; Yoder 2005).

Some go further and argue that the individual sayings are thought-provoking on their own. People do not realize this because they do not know how the genre works. Proverbs only look like platitudes without their performance context. As soon as we use them creatively in a given life-situation, they come alive (Vayntrub 2019:169).

Others claim that even without performance contexts, proverbs have great depths. The terse style of proverbs, created by placing things next to each other as if their connection was obvious, can mislead interpreters. In fact, those connections are seldom obvious.

Hope drawn out   sickens mind
and tree of   life desire come [13.12] …

It seems obvious that a hope that is prolonged without actualization is depressing, that is, it makes the heart/mind (lēb) sick. But is it obvious? Doesn't hope keep one going? Is not the anticipation of fulfilment a support of the lēb that is more significant than any realization?

(Williams 1995:80)

Luchsinger also notes the succinct style. He compares it with advertising language (Luchsinger 2010:68–80). The aim is to be simple and memorable in order to effectively influence the listener. Although advertisements do not depict all nuances of reality and may be criticized for this, their effectiveness may serve noble purposes. Others also think that the simple, schematic nature of proverbs fits their purpose. According to Clifford, their black-and-white language is good for motivation (Clifford 2009:246–7). According to Frydrych, their simple, archetypical categories ('the righteous', 'the wicked') are good for grasping the basic, underlying patterns of life (Frydrych 2002:18–23).

Millar combines these points in her marvellous book on the openness of proverbs. Similarly to Luchsinger, Clifford and Frydrych, she explains how using paradigmatic character types, such as wise/foolish or righteous/wicked (the typical character pairs in sentence literature), can be an effective means of character formation (Millar 2020:89–110). Similarly to Williams, she highlights how seemingly obvious statements are often open to different interpretations. This openness makes it possible to use the same proverb in different situations (Millar 2020:223), which is basically the point emphasized by Vayntrub above.

Many have recognized that the same proverb can serve different purposes in different situations (for example, Fox 2003:153; Weeks 2010:27), but it is seldom realized how far this can go. Folk proverbs are often used ironically, turning their meaning upside down (Vargha and Litovkina 2013). Millar mentions other factors that create openness, such as leaving evaluation to the reader:

> [16.14a:] 'The anger of the king – messenger of death'. … The reader might stand in awe, finding a paradigm for her own domestic dominion. Or she may be outraged, standing above the king in the moral hierarchy and condemning his murderous wrath (cf. 16:32).
>
> (Millar 2020:188)

Sometimes a proverb's *cola* may not match perfectly, making the reader ponder ('elliptical sayings', 'disjointed proverbs', 'imprecise parallelism' or 'imbalanced proverbs' in the literature; Clifford 2004:158–9; Fox 2004; Heim 2013:683; Millar Forthcoming).

> [10.16:] 'The wage of the righteous – to life; the produce of the wicked – to sin.' … in the second colon … we meet not the anticipated antithesis of 'life' (i.e., 'death,') but 'sin'. … The b colon may suggest that the wicked man gets ever more engrossed in sin, progressing through grades of wickedness … until it consumes his whole lifestyle and encapsulates his character. … Through the parallelism, the reader connects this sinful behavior with death. … [But the reader may also argue that] the absence of 'death' is conspicuous

and perhaps significant. In the balance of justice, retribution is expected but does not occur. The wicked are not, in fact, greeted with death.

(Millar 2020:123–5)

Fox agrees that a proverb can have different applications, but, he argues, proverbs still have a basic meaning that is stable:

> In a collection, a proverb has a fairly stable semantic core which is communicated to most readers; otherwise it would be useless in further interactions. Its performance meaning, however, exists only as a potential. A proverb is thus like a coin, whose value is definable but remains latent until the coin is spent on something, whereupon it can be said to have 'performance value.'

(Fox 2003:153)

Millar, at least occasionally, seems to suggest that even the basic meaning is unstable. Through the polysemy of some words (words carrying multiple meanings), grammatical equivocation (grammar allowing multiple meanings), ambiguity of imagery and ellipses (missing words), proverbs can often mean more than one thing (Millar 2020 throughout, but see pp. 66–72 about the limits of openness). Openness has benefits beyond making a proverb easier to use in different situations. It also trains the reader's thinking. The openness of a proverb means that some of its meanings lie far beneath its surface, so its readers have to 'climb in' and 'explore, further opening [it] up … for themselves' (Millar 2020:6). They are forced to use logic, imagination and self-reflection and to tolerate ambiguity. Therefore, one of the secrets of interpreting individual proverbs well lies in avoiding anxious efforts to find the only right interpretation and in interpreting them 'courageously' (Millar 2020:225), being open to hear non-dominant voices beneath the seemingly obvious meaning.

The authority of proverbs

> Aphorisms are essentially an aristocratic genre. … The aphorist does not argue or explain, he [sic] asserts; and implicit in his assertion is a conviction that he is wiser or more intelligent than his readers.

(Auden and Kronenberger 1962:VII–VIII)

Some think that, unlike aphorisms according to Auden and Cronenberg, biblical proverbs are one of the least imperious genres in the Bible.

The admonition of the wise man remains in the framework of counselling. …
Counsel affords a certain margin of liberty and of proper decision. Certainly
we cannot say that counsel has no authority. It has the authority of insight.
But that is quite different from the authority of the Lord, who decrees.

(Zimmerli 1964:153; similarly Crenshaw 2019:89)

Zimmerli thinks that a proverb, by definition, can only ask for but not
demand the reader's consent. Others, however, do not think proverbs are so
different from other biblical genres in terms of authority.

[Counsel] does not mean simply giving advice which can then be accepted
or rejected according to the whims of the hearer. When given as counsel, it is
the divine word no less than torah or oracle. Not surprisingly, then, 'mashal'
can mean 'oracle' as well as 'proverb'. … In this sense, wisdom is authoritative
dabhar, the word of Yahweh.

(Kovacs 1974:184–5; quoted affirmingly in Sneed 2015a:254)

Thus, the spectrum is ranging from those who think that proverbs allow
readers to judge their truth value (Zimmerli) to those who think that they
claim as much authority as the prophetic word (Kovacs and Sneed).

Pinpointing the source of their authority (whatever its measure) is not
straightforward. Scholars have offered many options:

- **Tradition**. If the sayings in Proverbs are folk proverbs or at least
  dependent on folk proverbs, they implicitly claim the authority
  of tradition and the wisdom of many generations (van Heerden
  2002:465).
- **Currency**. Widely known proverbs gain authority from broad social
  support (Sneed 2015a:191).
- **Unequivocal claims**. Proverbs lack discursive reasoning. Their
  'unapologetic immediacy' generates almost automatic acceptance
  of their claims. 'Rather than reflection leading to a conclusion, the
  conclusion comes first with an aphorism. Discerning how it is true (for
  it *must* be true) is the task of future contemplation' (Millar 2020:37).
- **Heightened style**. Elegance of expression gives proverbs power (Millar
  2020:36–7).
- **Writing**. Where the literacy level is low, the medium of writing conveys
  a sense of authority (see Vayntrub 2016:113, 2019:184).
- **Revelation**. Parts of Proverbs appeal to revelation. Lady Wisdom
  claims divine knowledge (chapter 8). The Solomonic titles (1.1; 10.1;
  25.1) allude to his divine gift of wisdom (1 Kgs 3.11-12). Proverbs 30.1
  and 31.1 may refer to oracles (Sneed 2015a:254–5, 312–13).

- **Authoritative speakers**. Solomon (1.1; 10.1; 25.1), parents (1.8; 6.20, etc.) and illustrious people (30.1; 31.1) lend their authority to proverbs (Weeks 2016:16). In a performance situation the speaker gives a proverb authority ('My mother … expressed her truths with so much authority that one accepted her sayings as Bible truths'; van Heerden 2002:465).
- **Experience**. What a proverb says may match the experience of the reader.
- **Performance situation**. Sayings may gain authority by strikingly fitting the situation in which they are used (25.11).
- **Modesty**. Because proverbs do not claim authority in every situation (see Millar 2020:208), one is inclined to bend to their authority when they do seem fitting (see previous point).

Therefore, their form (elegant, bold, written), literary context (Solomonic, divine) and performance context (well-known, traditional, well-chosen, used by authoritative speakers) make proverbs authoritative. Yet they are not oppressive as their openness demands their audience's wise interpretation.

Dating

While the absolute dating of individual proverbs is impossible, many scholars, especially in the second half of the twentieth century, argued that a temporal order between categories of proverbs could be established. They claimed that the earliest humanistic proverbs focused on the practicalities of life, while later proverbs were characterized by a Yahwistic pietism and a mechanical antithesis of the righteous and the wicked (see Fox 1968; McKane 2970:10–22; Scott 1972; Westermann 1995:75–84; and more tentatively Whybray 1965:72–104, 1979).

Recent research has raised questions about such theories. While the righteous/wicked antithesis is indeed different from the supposedly older wise/fool one, it is hardly more mechanical or less rooted in real life (Millar 2020:89–110). Also, it seems unlikely that the YHWH sayings, in general, are late. There are no signs of such religious reinterpretation in Egyptian or Mesopotamian writings. It sounds anachronistic to presuppose the existence of a 'secular' older wisdom (for further critique of the theory of late 'Yahwehization', see Schwáb 2013c:50–2).

Interpretation of sayings

Many think that the immediate literary context should guide the interpretation of a saying. It might have originally existed as an independent proverb, but it is now part of a carefully edited book. In Proverbs, the argument goes, sayings are arranged into clusters that focus on a single topic. Some clusters are obvious, but even if they are not, a skilled interpreter is able to recognize them and interpret their sayings accordingly (see the various attempts to find such clusters in Bellis 2018; Bryce 1979; Goldingay 1994; Heim 2001; Hermisson 1968; Hoglund 1987; Overland 2022; Waltke 2004, 2005; on proverbial pairs, see Hildebrandt 1988). Schipper argues that entire chapters are 'masterful compositions', not always in the sense of having a single point, but in contrasting and connecting different views on the same subject (Schipper 2019a:354–5).

Others argue that recent paremiological studies have affirmed (see Nahkola 2016) that a proverb, by definition, is independent. Interpretation should not kill it by 'freezing' its meaning with reference to the literary context (Longman III 2006:40; McKane 2970:413–14; Millar 2020:40–3; von Rad 1972:6; Westermann 1995:123). Of course, it is undeniable that there are chains of sayings in Proverbs. See, for example, the YHWH sayings in 16.1-9. But it is questionable whether the interpretation of 16.5 should be influenced by 16.1-4, 6-9. Often chains of sayings seem to be based on trivial associations; for example, the same key words are used without any substantial connection between the meanings (Weeks 1999:20–40). Therefore, we should not interpret a proverb with a view to its neighbours any more than we would interpret a joke in a joke book with a view to its neighbours (Weeks 2010:30).

There are also some who try to navigate between these two approaches and argue that it is worth taking clusters into account, even if a cluster cannot fix the meaning of a saying. If clusters provide interesting questions that stimulate thought, why should we ignore them? (See Schwáb 2013b; Kimilike 2018:146.)

Besides the question of whether the immediate context should, must not, or may be taken into consideration, there is also the question of the wider context. A saying may be related to many other sayings in the book. There are sayings that are repeated, albeit with slight variations (Heim 2013; Snell 1993). Key concepts such as 'righteousness' or 'wisdom' are used with remarkable consistency in the sayings, creating links between proverbs. Many sayings seem to contradict each other, some in close proximity (26.4-

5) and others further apart (see discussion above, in the section 'Boring or thought-provoking?'). Therefore, Proverbs is an intricate network of all sorts of connections which can influence the interpretation of a given saying.

Inevitably, I use a theory of interpretation in my following comments on the sayings, which should be revealed here. Even though I am happy to read the sayings in the light of each other, whether they are in close proximity or far away, I do not insist on finding clusters everywhere. Some clusters are unmistakable, but the sentence literature is often rather chaotic, lacking clearly defined clusters. But it is not completely without patterns. In the chaotic waters of the sea, waves can be detected. Similarly, in the chaotic sea of proverbial sayings, key themes emerge and fade away. Sometimes they clash, like the waves of the ocean. There are also undercurrents in the sea whose effects are only visible to the discerning eye. Similarly, in the sentence literature, we may sense the undercurrents of basic concerns below the waves of themes. Therefore, I will highlight some waves of themes and undercurrents of basic concerns, without the slightest intention of being comprehensive. Can anyone describe the ocean perfectly?

A personal excursus: Swimming in the sea

Researching the sea is important, but swimming in it is the real fun. If my readers want to swim in the sea of proverbs, my suggestion is to learn some consecutive sayings by heart. Different parts of the Bible suit different uses. Psalms should be sung. Stories should be imagined, inhabited and discussed. Sayings should be memorized. As we saw in Part I, this is an old practice dating back to ancient Near Eastern education systems.

In preparation for writing this book, I learned Proverbs 10 by heart, a verse a day (well, sometimes a verse a week). I also spent time every week studying the written text and meditating on possible connections between the sayings. It was hard work, but an unforgettable experience. These verses keep coming to mind when I read other parts of the Bible, have discussions with friends or just travel on the bus. I will never forget the excitement I felt when I realized that 10.4 ('A slack [or deceitful] hand causes poverty, but the hand of the diligent enriches') can be understood, at least on its own, to teach not only that the diligent will become rich but that diligent people enrich others while deceitful/lazy people impoverish others.

One of the effects of this exercise was that I started to feel the pull of righteousness. I am a great admirer of the English ideal of a gentleman (see Newman 1852), though I also have ambiguous feelings about it. But thanks to this exercise, a new ideal was born in my heart: the righteous (see Lyu 2012). I often found myself soul-searching whether my smiling face hid any hatred or violence (10.6b, 11b, 18a), or whether my words foolishly revealed my hatred (10.18b). Did my speech bring life to others (10.11a) and did my love cover their sins (10.12b)? However conventional and boring the schematic image of the righteous person may look in chapter 10, I found myself wanting to be one. This is probably not far from the intended purpose of the chapter.

I also experienced the difficulties of students in antiquity. Carr writes about these difficulties:

> The Satiric Letter [an Egyptian writing from the Ramesside Period] indicates that such memorization was not easy, particularly when it came to keeping the various sayings in order. ... The speaker criticizes another's faulty knowledge of a saying he quoted, not knowing 'which stanza is before it, which after it', and manuscripts with variant orders of sayings testify to the possible rearrangement of items in tradents' memories.
>
> (Carr 2005:72)

Quite so. Remembering the order of sayings is a nightmare. The trick was to remember the initial words in order. Also, it was difficult to remember *colon* B when it did not match *colon* A – but this forced me to meditate on possible connections between the two. Recurring words, playful sound patterns and rhythms also helped me. In 10.23a, for example, the Hebrew which, at least for me, functions as a tongue-twister made it easy to remember.

Thus, if you want to feel the waves of the proverb-ocean and the agonies of scribal students, memorize some proverbs.

10.1–22.16

The title 'Proverbs of Solomon' (10.1a) is noteworthy. In Hebrew the two words share the same consonants: *mishley shlomoh*. It may even contain a riddle, as the numerical value of 'Solomon' (the sum of the numeric values traditionally assigned to its Hebrew letters) happens to be 375, the exact number of sayings in 10.1–22.16 (Skehan 1948:117).

In 10.1–15.33 predominantly antithetical parallelisms are presented ('A wise son makes his father rejoice; a foolish son: his mother's grief' (10.1)), contrasting the righteous with the wicked, the wise with the fool and other minor characters. In 16.1–22.16 more synonymous parallelisms ('Irritation to his father, a foolish son; and bitterness to her who bore him' (17.25)) and images are used. The central role of YHWH is indicated by the high number of YHWH sayings in the middle (chapters 15 and 16).

Chapters 10–15

Chapters 10–12

Chapters 10–11 focus on the righteous/wicked contrast. We learn that righteousness pays well, but the real emphasis is on what righteousness saves a person from. For example, it delivers from death (10.2b; see also 11.3-8). This emphasis on avoiding danger and destruction is prevalent throughout Proverbs. Other themes that appear right at the beginning and run through the whole collection include the value of material wealth, accepting discipline, the importance of hard work and graciousness towards the unfortunate (11.15-17, 24-26; 12.10). Most prominent of all is the power and right use of speech. It is a matter of life and death. Speech can destroy speakers (10.8b = 10.10b) and people around them (10.6b = 10.11b; 10.14b), but it can also give life and feed others (10.11a, 21a). The godless deliberately use speech to destroy their neighbours (11.9) or even whole cities (11.11), whereas the tongue of the wise brings healing (12.18). Right speech provides food (10.21; 12.14; 13.2), reminding us of Deuteronomy 8.3 (and Mt.44; Lk. 47), 'a human being does not live on bread only but on everything that leaves the mouth of YHWH'. Proverbs goes further: even human words are nourishing if they are well chosen.

Chapter 13

The tone begins to change. Familiar themes are repeated (the value of wealth: 13.7, 8, 11, 22, 23; speech: 13.2, 3; safety: 13.14, 15), but the righteous/wicked contrast is less dominant (it occurs in 13.5, 6, 9, 21, 25). The topic of listening (13.1, 8, 10, 13, 14, 18, 24) is important along with desire, a topic that is not new (10.3) but especially emphasized here (13.2, 4, 12, 19, 25).

The word *nephesh* occurs seven times. It is usually translated as 'life' or 'spirit', but it can also mean 'desire'. In 13.2b 'the desire (*nephesh*) of the treacherous [is for] violence' and in 13.4 the desire (*nephesh*) of the lazy 'craves but has nothing'. In between is 13.3: 'He who watches his mouth guards his life (*nephesh*); he who opens his lips wide – disaster is his.' It makes sense to translate *nephesh* as 'life' here, but due to its neighbours, the verse may also indicate the secret of taming unruly desires: those who talk less guard their desires. Interestingly, the first Hebrew letters of the words in this verse in sequence produce *nepheshnephesh*.

Chapter 14

Starting in chapter 13, the wise/foolish antithesis gradually overshadows the righteous/wicked one. In chapter 14, foolishness is a major theme. The word *iwwelet* ('folly', 'foolish') occurs seven times (14.1, 8, 17, 18, 24 [x2], 29). Another major theme is the relationship between appearance and reality. There are ways that appear right but lead to death (14.12). The simple and the fool are easily misled by appearances (14.8, 15). Just as the direction of a path, the inner world of humans can be hidden. Those who laugh may be crying inside (14.13). Only the heart knows its own bitterness; strangers cannot see it (14.10).

Chapter 15

But YHWH is not a stranger. He sees human hearts and he judges accordingly. This is a major theme in chapter 15, with its many YHWH sayings (15.3, 8, 9, 11, 16, 25, 26, 29, 33). The fear of YHWH, humility and the ability to listen are often mentioned (15.5, 10, 12, 31-33). The theme of speech is also picked up, this time with an emphasis on giving an answer (see 15.1, 2, 4, 7, 23, 28). This theme kicks off in 15.1, which is particularly striking if read with the last verse of chapter 14: '(The king's) wrath falls on one who acts shamefully. A soft answer turns away wrath' (14.35b-15.1a). A soft answer overpowers the king himself! Gentle words are as powerful as the tree of life (15.4). No wonder a good answer is something the righteous are always searching for (15.23, 28).

Chapters 16–22

Chapter 16

We might search for the perfect answer, but only YHWH can give it, states the first verse. This is the first of a series of verses that are about YHWH's activity (16.1-9, 11). Besides giving answers, these verses mention key themes from the previous chapter, such as the way (16.2, 9) and appearance versus reality (16.2). God sees, judges and controls everything. Following the discussion of God's power, we turn to the power of the king (16.10, 12-15). His judgements, wrath and favour are reminiscent of those of YHWH. Whether this means that the king represents YHWH or is a rival is a matter of interpretation (Millar 2020:159–90).

The rest of the chapter discusses virtues (mainly 16.16-24) and vices (mainly 16.25-30), so there seems to be a movement from YHWH to the king and then to ordinary people (Fox 2009:605). The midpoint of Proverbs happens to be here (16.17). It emphasizes the importance of guarding one's way. Reading it with 16.18-19 suggests that this 'way' includes thoughts and feelings, not only actions.

The importance of persuasiveness is a significant theme in 16.16-33. The wise seek sweet, persuasive words (16.21, 23, 24) but worthless people can also be persuasive. Their violent power can be appealing (16.29) but their words are dangerous like fire (16.27). In particular, they generate strife (16.28). Sowing strife is one of the main sins in Proverbs (3.30; 10.12; 13.10; 15.18; 17.1, 9, 14, 19; 18.6, 19; 19.13; 20.3; 21.9, 19; 22.10; 23.29; 25.24; 26.17, 20-21; 27.15; 28.25; 29.8, 22; 30.33; the topic of hiding hatred and violence with flattering words is related; see 10.6, 11-12, 18; 16.29; 26.23-28). This may surprise modern readers, but think, for example, of the destructive power of workplace gossip today. Conversely, pacifying others and avoiding quarrels by being cool-headed is a major virtue (15.1, 18; 16.14, 32; 19.11).

Chapter 17

Proverbs 17.1 contains a graphic description of the seriousness of strife: 'Better is a dry morsel with tranquillity than a house full of feasting with strife.' The chapter contains other well-known and influential verses. For instance, 17.5a ('Those who mock the poor insult their Maker'; see also 22.2) has often been lauded as a biblical foundation of human rights (Bloom 1954; Doll 1985:85; Golka 1993:121; Mariottini 2014; Westermann 1998:86–7). The theme of fools may be the most prominent in the chapter (17.10, 12, 16, 21, 24-25). It is hard to teach them and they are dangerous. What is emphasized here (unlike in 1.32; 3.35; or 18.7) is not that they ruin themselves but that they are a threat to others ('Encounter a bear bereft of her young, but not a fool in his folly' (17.12); for fools as a threat, see also 13.20; 14.7-8; 19.13; 26.6, 10).

Chapter 18

In this chapter the themes of strife and fools are related: 'The lips of the fool go into strife' (18.7), which is unsurprising. Fools are very opinionated: 'A fool is not delighted by understanding but only by disclosing his mind (literally "heart")' (18.2). The chapter also addresses issues such as the power of speech (18.4, 8, 20-21), finding a good wife (18.22) and friendship (18.24). Some themes are organized into loose clusters; for example, 18.10-12 discusses real or false security, and all the verses in 18.16-19 can be related to legal debates. But it is also fun to connect sayings across clusters. Of course fools are keen to reveal their thoughts (18.2) because they are proud ('Before destruction a man's heart grows haughty' (18.12)) and this is why they are unable to listen ('Answering before one listens, that is his folly and disgrace' (18.13)). Over-confident scholars, take note of these warnings!

Chapter 19

Proverbs 19.1-10 has a great deal to say about fools, the poor and the rich. In 19.11-29 we read about several other characters too, such as the king, wives, God and parents with their discipline. A person's relationship with these characters may seal their fate. Throughout the chapter we read about different causes of disasters. False witness is punished (19.5, 9), laziness causes hunger (19.15), neglecting commandments leads to death (19.16) and violence attracts trouble (19.19). Does this mean that being poor results from being violent, lazy, heedless and mendacious? Not necessarily, because it is possible to be poor and have integrity (19.1, 22b). The poor even represent God (19.17). So why are good people poor then? It is hard to be certain beyond stating that everything is in God's hands (19.14, 21). But be careful, because it is the custom of fools to blame God for their bad luck (19.3).

Chapter 20

This chapter discusses various topics: mockers and fools (20.1, 3); laziness (20.4, 13); dishonest measures (20.10, 23); the power of good and irresponsible speech (20.5, 18-20, 25) and so on. The knowledge and power of the king (20.2, 8, 26, 28) and God (20.12, 24, 27), especially in judging people, are mentioned regularly. In contrast, ordinary people should recognize their limitations. They can easily misjudge themselves (20.6); they cannot cleanse their hearts (20.9, though see 20.30) and cannot comprehend their own life (20.24).

Chapter 21

The king who possesses almost divine power in chapter 20 is suddenly put in his place in 21.1 ('Like streams of water is the king's heart in YHWH's hand, he bends it wherever he wishes'). In fact, we are all put in our place at both ends of the chapter: the Lord weighs human hearts; no human wisdom or power matters because only his decisions matter (21.1-3, 30-31). The juxtaposition of the king and YHWH and their powers in chapters 20–21 is reminiscent of 16.1-15 in the centre of the section. The wicked/

righteous antithesis becomes dominant, as in chapters 10–12. But there is still room for other characters, such as the diligent (21.5), the lazy (21.25), the proud (21.24) and the poor (21.13). The contentious wife also returns, gradually driving her unfortunate husband out from under the 'leaking roof' (19.13) to the roof itself (21.9) and then even into the desert (21.19).

22.1-16

A number of motives from chapters 1–9 return. The simple are compared with the clever (22.3; in 1.4 the simple are taught cleverness); the young are taught (22.6; see 1.4); the fear of YHWH provides riches, honour and life (22.4; see 1.7; 3.16; 8.13; 9.10); and the choice between good and bad is emphasized (22.5-6; see 2.15). Even the strange woman reappears (22.14; see 2.16). But instead of ending on any of these familiar motifs, 10.1–22.16 ends on an enigmatic verse about oppressing the poor. The verse literally states 'oppressing the poor to increase for him, giving to the rich only to neediness'. As Bellis (2018:211) explains, this can mean at least four things:

1) Oppressing the poor will enrich the poor; giving to the rich will impoverish the giver
2) Oppressing the poor will enrich the oppressor; giving to the rich will impoverish the rich
3) Oppressing the poor will enrich the poor; giving to the rich will impoverish the rich
4) Oppressing the poor will enrich the oppressor; giving to the rich will impoverish the giver.

This is an appropriate ending, given the many sayings about the poor and the rich (see 22.1, 2, 7, 9 in this chapter alone). It is also appropriate to end with a riddle to test whether the reader has mastered the art of interpretation (see 1.6).

22.17–24.22

This section switches back to longer instructions. There are parental exhortations, commandments and prohibitions, followed by motive clauses. This is not unlike chapters 1–9, although the instructions here are shorter. There are further similarities in both language and content. The son should incline his ears to the father's teaching (22.17; see 5.1); the purpose of the teaching is a good relationship with YHWH (22.17-21; see 1.1-7); the strange woman appears (23.27-28; see chapters 5–7); and wisdom, understanding and knowledge are used to create a house/the universe (24.3-4; see 3.19-20, van Leeuwen 2007). Thus, there may be a connection with chapters 1–9, but it is hard to be certain about the direction of influence (Dell 2006:74–5).

The section has two stated purposes. The first is to make good emissaries (22.21). This may sound rather irrelevant to modern readers, but emissaries were crucial in that time (see 10.26; 13.17; 17.11; 25.13). High-ranking emissaries had the responsibility of achieving the aims of their masters (Fox 2009:712–13; Whybray 1994a:328). The second stated purpose is to generate trust in YHWH (22.19). It is not absolutely clear what generates that trust. Perhaps the logic is that readers are encouraged not to envy and join evildoers in their unethical and apparently efficient methods (23.17; 24.1, 19). They should trust YHWH to bless their seemingly less effectual honest and ethical behaviour. We are warned repeatedly that although evildoers may seem successful, the future belongs to the God-fearing wise people (23.17-18; 24.13-14, 19-20). However, some readers may wonder how the last instruction (24.21-22) about fearing YHWH and kings because they can ruin the reader contributes to building trust in YHWH.

22.17–23.11

The title 'words of the wise' (22.17) is surprising. In the ancient Near East, teachings were usually attributed to famous individuals. The speaker later uses the first-person singular (22.19: 'I have made them known to you'). While the teacher conveys the reliable wisdom of past ages, he himself remains in the background.

The Hebrew of 22.20 is awkward. It is usually reconstructed to refer to 'thirty sayings'. The main reason for this is the connection with the Egyptian *Instructions of Amenemope* (see Ancient Near Eastern parallels in Part I), which has thirty sayings. The actual number of sayings in 22.17–24.22 seems to be short of thirty, but some still try to divide the text into thirty units (for one such attempt, see Fox 2009:705). Mainly 22.17–23.11 is similar to *Amenemope*, the rest (23.12–24.22) may have been influenced by other ancient Near Eastern writings (Fox 2009:706, 753–69).

23.12–24.22

Some think that 23.12–24.22 has a 'courtly' nature (Sneed 2015a:189); others argue that some mentions of rulers (22.29; 23.1-3) do not necessarily make it 'courtly' (Weeks 2010:34).

It has several memorable instructions. It is hard to miss the entertaining poetry of 23.29-35 describing drunkenness. The alcoholic is in the process of waking up and is struggling with a hangover. He feels seasick and notices his bruises (but cannot remember how he got them), yet his first thought is to find another drink. For other reasons 24.10-12 is also striking. In a book that emphasizes avoiding danger, it is refreshing to read an instruction to be brave and rescue others. Again, 24.17-18 is eye-catching. It cautions against rejoicing over an enemy's misfortune because YHWH may respond by ending it. It is hard to decide whether this instruction is about how to love your enemy or how to cause them as much suffering as possible.

24.23-34

This section is usually described as an appendix containing miscellaneous proverbs: three verses on impartiality in legal judgments (24.23b-25), one on honest answers (24.26), one on working one's field before building a house (24.27), two against taking revenge by bearing false witness (24.28-29; though not everyone thinks these verses are related, see van Leeuwen 1997:213–14) and a longer anecdote about laziness (24.30-34). However, since two broader topics are interwoven here – honest speech in a legal context (24.23-26, 28-29) and diligent work (24.26-27, 30-34) – it is no more miscellaneous than the previous sections.

The sayings about speech teach honesty, both when it is tempting to be nice to the wicked because they are important or friends (24.23-26) and when it is tempting to be unjust to the innocent because they are enemies. Honesty is as good an expression of love as a kiss ('he kisses lips, who answers with honest words' (24.26)).

The general message about diligence is obvious, but some details are opaque. Does working a field before building a house (24.27) mean that one should prepare before embarking on major projects; do their duty in terms of their father's property before gaining independence; establish finances before getting married; work hard before enjoying family life; or secure a source of income before making a public display of riches? Whatever the case, the saying teaches 'first things first' (compare Fox 2009:772; Longman III 2006:442; Steinberg 2019:191; Weeks 2010:35). As for 24.30-34, the conclusion contains a striking personification. Poverty is like a 'vagabond' (or 'robber'; compare Fox 2009:773, 2000:217) and an 'armed warrior'. The metaphor is open to various interpretations. Is the onset of poverty fast and unexpected, merciless, first hidden ('robber') and then obvious ('warrior'), temporary (robbers and warriors do not stay forever), or some combination of these?

25.1–29.27

Like 10.1–22.16, this collection contains sayings about a great variety of topics. The first verse attributes it to 'Hezekiah's men' who lived towards the end of the eighth century BCE. Unfortunately, we do not know who those men were (see Ansberry 2011:127) and what they did with the proverbs, as the Hebrew term is opaque. Did they copy them (NRSV), collect them, transmit them, separate them, interpret them or put them into writing (Fox 2009:777; Vayntrub 2019:80, 197–8; Weeks 2010:26)? In any case, the title suggests a royal provenance and indeed, rulers are frequently mentioned (25.1-7; 28.15-16; 29.4, 12, 14).

Some think that the collection contains training material for princes or royal courtiers, but this is debated (compare Ansberry 2011:128–9; Bryce 1979; Fox 2009:775-6, 817–19; Humphreys 1978; van Leeuwen 1988; Longman III 2006:487; Malchow 1985; Skladny 1962; Tavares 2007). It contains easily detectable clusters, for instance, sayings about the king in 25.2-7 and speech-related sayings in 25.11-15. The sayings are longer than in 10.1–22.16 and contain many metaphors and similes. Often, the first line contains an image ('Clouds and wind but no rain' (25.14a)) followed by an explanation ('a man boasting about a disappointing gift' (25.14b)). These sayings sound like riddles with solutions (Fox 2009:775–6). The collection has two parts: chapters 25–26 and 27–29. The former has more clusters, admonitions and images; the latter contains more antithetical proverbs and references to YHWH.

Chapters 25–26

Kings like to search out God's secrets (25.2), but ordinary folk cannot search out the minds of kings (25.3). Since this collection has been created by the king's men (25.1), we can hope it contains some divine secrets discovered by kings. One secret seems to be that self-control is crucial to a good life. Not being pushy in the royal court (25.6-7), not revealing secrets in legal courts (25.8-10), not raising one's voice in a debate (25.15), not visiting friends too often (25.16-17) and not seeking honour by any means (25.27;

the translation is debated; see Fox 2015a:339–40; Longman III 2006:459–60) are all beneficial but demand self-control. Without it we are like a breached city (25.28). Chapter 25 also talks about annoying, painful people (25.14, 18-22, 23-24) and people who refresh one's spirit (25.11-13, 25).

Chapter 26 begins with a cluster of proverbs about fools (26.1-12), including a famous contradiction 'Do not answer fools … Answer fools' (26.4-5). As there are so many fools around us, it would be important to know whether we should answer them. Many have attempted to solve this riddle (van Heerden 2008; Heim 2010; Hoglund 1987; Schwáb 2016; Sneed 2015a:273). However, if anyone finds the solution, they should not be too proud of their wisdom because those who are wise in their own eyes are worse than fools (26.12). The next cluster (26.13-16) is about lazy people, who also think that they are very clever (compare 26.5 and 26.16). The following clusters are about quarrelsome people (26.17-22) and false friends (26.23-28).

Chapters 27–29

Some verses in chapter 27 offer insights into the cravings and aches of the human soul (see 27.8-9, 20), but most focus on human relationships in society. For instance, 'A crucible is for silver and a furnace is for gold and a man [is tested] by the mouth of one who is praising him' (27.21). We should leave the task of praising us to others (17.2), but when that praise comes, it is a great challenge to moral integrity. (For the dangers of the enemies' niceties, see 27.5-6.) After numerous perceptive comments, the chapter ends in a little epigram about the superiority of animal husbandry compared to hoarding goods (27.23-27). In relation to the king, this is a metaphor for taking care of one's people and serves as a good introduction to chapters 28-29 with their royal sayings (but see Fox's cautious approach to metaphorical readings of this epigram in Fox 2009:814–16).

Chapter 28 talks about rulers, the rich and the poor. It is important to understand the value and methods of justice (28.5; see 29.7) and one should not use all conceivable means to become rich (28.20, 22, 24) because righteousness and integrity will prevail (28.1, 7, 9, 10, 12, 13, 18, 26). This does not mean that the wicked will never be successful (28.6, 12, 28), but they will ultimately perish (28.28) and the righteous will inherit their riches (28.8). Interestingly, 28.3a speaks about poor people who oppress other poor people. Many emend the Hebrew so that the 'ruler', the 'rich' or the 'wicked' are the oppressors (Bellis 2018:238).

The themes of chapter 28 continue into chapter 29, although we read less about the rich and more about the righteous. There are several verses about ruling well (29.4, 14) and how it can go wrong: wicked rulers are like raging bears, permit economic injustice and foster court intrigues (29.2, 12, 16, 18; see also 28.3, 15-16, 28). But many of the issues in chapter 29 apply to everyone, for example, hasty speech (29.20), anger which stirs up strife (29.22) and discipline (29.15, 17, 19, 21). Towards the end of the chapter, the secret of true bravery (which according to 28.1 characterizes the righteous) is revealed; it is trust in God: 'The fear of man lays a snare [for the man], but he who trusts in YHWH will be secure' (29.25; see 14.26).

30.1-33

The title ('The words of Agur son of Jakeh') is not very revealing as we do not know anything about Agur. The next Hebrew word either means 'oracle' (NRSV) or describes Agur's provenance, 'the Massaite', referring to an Arabian tribe (Gen. 25.14; 1 Chron. 1.30). The rest of 30.1 is 'virtual gibberish' (Weeks 2010:43). Scholars debate if the key word is a name, 'Ithiel', or should be translated as 'There is no God', 'I am not God', 'God is with him', 'I am weary, God' or 'I am an idiot' (see Fogielman 2019; Kirk 2022; Sandoval 2020a).

This enigmatic first verse is followed by a confession that the author is as stupid as a brute animal (30.2-3) – quite a statement within the context of Proverbs (compare 30.3 with 9.10). The questions in 30.4 suggest that other human beings have no reason to boast either, since no one has access to the secrets of the universe, but 30.5-6 is consoling: God's word, which reveals at least some secrets, is reliable. The only prayer in Proverbs is found in 30.7-9. It is a prayer for protection against the one who prays himself. It expresses self-doubt, asking God not to grant too much or too little, as either would pose an irresistible temptation to neglect God.

A series of mostly numerical sayings follows (30.10-33). Many have a playful tone. This one is often quoted:

> Three things are too wonderful for me, four I do not understand: the way of the eagle in the sky, the way of a snake on a rock, the way of a ship in the middle of the sea, and the way of a man with a girl.
>
> (30.18-19)

What do these have in common? Is it that they leave no trace and are impossible to follow? Is it that the mechanics of their movements seem impossible? Is it that their movements are graceful? Is it that they belong to different spheres (air, earth, water, love – the spiritual sphere)? In any case, all of them are wonderful unlike the way of the adulteress described next: 'she eats, wipes her mouth and says "I have done no wrong"' (30.20). The last saying (30.32-33) insists that if anyone has been foolish, proud or evil, he should be quiet – and then the speaker is quiet.

It is not easy to determine where Agur's words end. Some think that his sceptical voice ends in 30.4 and what follows are pious additions. Others take 30.1-9 as his words, or 30.1-14, or the whole chapter (see Fox 2009:851). The whole chapter is characterized by a 'colourful quirkiness' (Weeks 2010:44) that is simultaneously appealing and challenging to interpreters. Besides the translation issues in 30.1b, it is debated whether Agur is a sceptic who doubts basic biblical teachings or a pious person with a deep trust in God, whether his scepticism about obtaining wisdom (30.4) challenges the teaching of the rest of Proverbs or simply embodies the 'do-not-be-wise-in-your-own-eyes' humility (3.7; 26.12), and whether he argues that Torah piety is superior to wisdom or equates wisdom with the Torah (compare Brown 2019:72–74; Camp 2015:33, 36; Franklyn 1983; Kline 2021; Moore 1994; O'Dowd 2019; Schipper 2021:268–74; Yoder 2009a).

31.1-31

We know nothing about Lemuel other than that he was from Massa, like Agur (alternatively, he had an oracle; see comment on 30.1). It is debated whether the poem in 31.10-31 belongs to Lemuel's teaching (compare Hurowitz 2001; Fox 2009:883).

Lemuel passes on the instruction of his mother. Her teaching, in 31.1-9, combines two important topics of Proverbs: warnings against destructive women (5–7; 9; 11.22; 12.4; 14.1; 19.13; 21.9, 19; 25.24; 27.15; 22.14; 30.20) and drunkenness (20:1; 21:17; 23:20-21, 29-35). According to Lemuel's mother, these are the two prime threats to a king.

But as the book's final song about the 'capable woman' shows, not all women are destructive (31.10-31). The Hebrew term for 'capable' (*hayil*) is usually applied to men. It means 'wealth' (1 Sam. 9.1; 2 Kgs 15.20) or 'might' (1 Sam. 14.52; 2 Sam. 11.16) or 'ability' (Exod. 18.25; 1 Kgs 11.28). A 'man of *hayil*' is able to achieve things due to his wealth, strength or talent. Here it is a 'woman of *hayil*' (see also 12.4). There is one 'woman of *hayil*' outside Proverbs, Ruth (Ruth 3.11), whose story follows Proverbs according to a common Jewish order of the biblical books (Dell 2019; Goswell 2019:15).

The woman manages industry (31.13), commerce (31.14), hospitality (31.15), agriculture (31.16), social care (31.20) and education (31.26) better than most governments. She pays special attention to her own and her family's clothes (31.21-24), but she is also clothed in strength and majesty (31.25). Ellen Davis notes that the poem 'demonstrates how different from Greek philosophical works … is the character of Israelite wisdom: practical, non-abstract, yet intellectually subtle and sound' (Davis 2019:336).

Some interpret the poem in the light of the social realities of women and estates in Persian Yehud, but others caution that it is hard to be certain what lies behind the poetic imagery (Ben Zvi 2015; Yoder 2003; for a critique of Yoder, see Fox 2009:900–2).

The passage is an acrostic poem whose twenty-two lines begin with the twenty-two letters of the Hebrew alphabet. Al Wolters notes that the poem has a hymnic style typically used to praise warriors or YHWH himself (Wolters 2001; see also Davis 2000:152–3). The woman is praised by her family for her fear of YHWH (31.30), recalling the motto at the beginning of the book (1.7) at the end. It has been suggested that the woman may be another personification of Lady Wisdom (McCreesh 1985) in which case the hymn is about a divine being rather than a flesh-and-blood woman. There may even be a covert hint at wisdom in 31.27, where the Hebrew has *tsophiyyah* ('she looks for') which sounds like the Greek word for wisdom, *sophia* (Wolters 2001:30–41). Although not everyone is persuaded that this is Lady Wisdom herself (Fox 2009:907–11; Waltke 2005:521), she at least reminds the readers of Lady Wisdom in the beginning of the book.

Anthology or book?

The book of Proverbs ranges from topic to topic, from recommendations regarding sexual conduct, advice on farming, rules of court etiquette to descriptions of superwomen, often with no obvious principle of organization. Does it function as a book? Hardly, argues Karel van der Toorn. Before Hellenism, he explains, there was no such thing as a 'book' in the modern sense. Scribes collected useful material to aid their memories, not to create works that would be read by the wider public for education or entertainment.

Even if Proverbs was given its final form during Hellenism, it preserved this anthological character. An anthology is not logical or analytical; it does not need seamless plot development but consists of juxtapositions, adding one opinion to another (van der Toorn 2007:5, 9, 15–16, 118–19).

Modern readers may find Proverbs frustrating. (This explains why so many popular and academic books rearrange their contents in topical order, for example, Davis (2010); Voorwinde (2012); Wax (2018); Woodcock (1988).) But anthologies have advantages, too. By presenting different opinions, they achieve a degree of comprehensiveness (see Vayntrub 2019:198). They provide freedom to the reader to rearrange the material without fear of ruining a tight structure. The haphazard order of the material also mirrors the haphazard order of human experience. In the real world, decisions about sex, work and etiquette are not neatly separated.

However, despite its anthological nature, Proverbs also has unity. Key concepts such as 'the fool' or 'the simple' are used consistently throughout the book. There are also links between the collections. Many proverbs, often with slight variations, are repeated, creating complex interconnections (for such twice-told proverbs, see Carr 2005:37; Fox 2015a:59; Heim 2013; Schipper 2019a:350–2; Snell 1993; Sneed 2019). The titles, when they indicate awareness of other parts of the book (24:23), suggest editorial activity to create connections between the units. The YHWH sayings that are placed at structurally key points also testify to such editorial activity (Whybray 1979, 1994b:76–8, 86–9, 150).

The clearest sign of editorial activity is the placement of the first nine chapters before the rest. It was a typical ancient Near Eastern (and biblical) method to place a prologue in front of a scribal collection, thereby creating a context for the whole work (Sanders 2017:8; van der Toorn 2007:257–8). The reference to the seven pillars of Wisdom's house in 9.1 may allude to the seven parts of Proverbs (Hurowitz 2001) and 1.1-7 also seems to presume all the later superscriptions in the book (Schipper 2019a:9). Keefer (2020) argues that chapters 1–9 provide guidance on how to interpret the sayings. It certainly encourages readers to adopt an attentive, submissive attitude (Millar 2020:38–39; see fear of YHWH in 1.7 and 9.10). By personifying Lady Wisdom, chapters 1–9 make it the object of our desire as we read about wisdom in the rest of the book (Camp 1985:167–78, 209–22).

A work with conceptual unity, with an introduction that prepares readers for what follows and with an ending that echoes the introduction (see discussion at Prov. 31 above), has more unity than an anthology with sections randomly placed next to each other. Mark Sneed (2015a:299), for example, sees alternation between longer instructions and shorter sentences: instructions (1–9), sentences (10–22), instructions (22–24), sentences (25–29) and instructions (30–31). Schipper (2019a: 4–5, 10) thinks the sections provide increasingly advanced teaching. Some scholars argue that Proverbs even has some plot development. According to Brown (1996:22–49, 2004:137), the book has a 'narrative arc'. It begins with a young boy looking for a wife (1–9) and ends with wisdom incarnate as the perfect wife (31.10-31). Brown (2002) also recognizes another related narrative arc. The book starts with a naive son and ends with a direct address to the king (31.1-9). But just as the young boy becomes a king and, presumably, readers gain royal characteristics as they learn wisdom, so the book also contains growing criticism of kings, thereby challenging readers to critical self-reflection and humility (see also Ansberry 2011; Yoder 2005).

World view of proverbs

Theology

Creation theology

The major religious themes of the Hebrew Bible, such as election, the exodus, the Sinai covenant and the temple, are missing from Proverbs. Religious practices such as prayer, sacrifice and prophecy are mentioned rarely and without the Israelite specifics (15.8, 29; 21.3, 27; 28.9; 29.18; 30.1, 7-9; 31.1). The words 'torah' and 'commandments' are frequently used, but it is debated whether they refer to the Mosaic Torah and commandments (see the discussion on Deuteronomy in Part III). Many think that creation is the only religious theme which plays an important role in Proverbs. The act of creation is described in some of the most powerful passages (3.19-20; 8) and elements of creation such as the animal world are an important source of metaphors and images (Forti 2008).

Ever since Zimmerli's influential statement that 'wisdom thinks resolutely within the framework of a theology of creation' (1964:148) it has been customary to refer to the 'creation theology' of Proverbs. For some, its main function is to recognize God in everyday life (Brueggemann 1996, 1997:333–58). Others see a special emphasis on beauty, metaphor and imagination (Perdue 1994:48) or on beauty and divine power (Schwáb 2022a).

Proverbs' creation theology has often been portrayed as an alternative to the typical salvation history (*Heilsgeschichte*) of the Old Testament (influentially, von Rad 1972). However, some caution that Proverbs does not present unified teaching about creation and it cannot be said to embody an alternative tradition, given that the theme of creation is pervasive throughout the Hebrew Bible (Boström 1990:80; Schwáb 2013c:60–1; Weeks 2010:111).

World order

The heart of creation theology, according to many, is the affirmation of order in the world. Hartmut Gese (1958) famously argued that the Egyptian deity *Ma'at*, who represented order and justice, was a model for Wisdom. Hans Heinrich Schmid (1966, 1968) claimed that world order (*Weltordnung*) was a key concept throughout the ancient Near East and that *tsedeq* (righteousness), which is a prominent concept in Proverbs, was an expression of it in Israelite thinking.

Klaus Koch (1955, 1983) suggested that the act–consequence connection (*Tun–Ergehen Zusammenhang*) is the mechanism through which the world order is maintained. This, according to Koch, is a quasi-automatic process. Instead of God inflicting rewards or punishments, consequences grow naturally from acts, like plants from seeds. God is like a gardener or midwife who only supports the birth of a consequence. Koch's idea has ruled the interpretation of Proverbs for decades, with slight modifications; for example, some have argued that it would be more precise to speak of the 'character–consequence connection' (Hildebrandt 1992:438) or 'attitude–fate connection' (Skladny 1962:71–5).

World order is still a frequently used concept in the interpretation of Proverbs (O'Dowd 2009:111–36; Schipper 2019b:23–4). However, some details of the Gese–Schmid–Koch description have been qualified. Neither Egyptian nor Israelite writings suggest that the world order operates automatically. The right world order has to be maintained by divine or human actions (Fox 1995). Millar writes:

> Many proverbs do speak of an active deity, who blesses (10:22; 16:20; 18:22), directs behavior (16:1, 9; 20:24), tests hearts (15:11; 17:3; 21:2), creates (16:4; 20:12; 22:2), and (despite Koch's protestations) administers rewards and punishments (12:2; 15:25; 16:5, 7; 17:5; 19:14, 17; 21:12; 22:12, 14, 22-23; 24:12).
>
> (Millar 2020:117; for the similar role of
> human society, see Janowski 1994)

Millar (2020:125, 155–6) also notes that some proverbs that seemingly affirm a correspondence between actions and consequences allow for discrepancies. Indeed, the connection between act and consequence is not inevitable in Proverbs. It regularly refers to people who suffer or succeed undeservedly ('Better a poor man walking in his integrity than one of crooked ways who is rich' (28.6); see also 13.23; 15.16-17; 16.8; 19; 17.1; 19.1, 22; 24.11-12; 28.15-16; 29.2; 30.14; see van Leeuwen 1992; Schwáb 2013c:58–9, 220–3).

Regularities and the power of God

The book of Proverbs places an emphasis on regularities, even if they are not completely inviolable. Righteousness is *usually* beneficial in material terms. In this respect, Fox's distinction between a 'predictable' and 'mechanistic' world order is helpful (1995:40–1).

The focus on predictable regularities is not there to explain what happens in the world in all places, to everyone, all the time. Instead, the purpose is motivational (van Leeuwen 1992; Millar 2020:118–19). Surely, when parents today tell their children to study to get ahead in life, they do not mean that every successful manager was once a diligent student and every beggar a lazy body. They use this language because there is *some* truth in it and they want to motivate their children.

Finally, whatever definition of world order one accepts, in Proverbs it is subject to an all-powerful God. Wisdom depends on fearing him (1.7; 9.10), he is the one who makes a person rich (10.22) and directs people's ways (16.9). Everything depends on him. Therefore, it may be better to speak about a creator theology than creation theology (Schwáb 2022a). Paradoxically, a great deal depends on human action, too. People should buy wisdom (4.5-7), work diligently to generate wealth (10.4) and pay attention to their ways (4.26).

Anthropology

Ideal human beings fear God (1.7, 29; 2.5; 3.7; 8.13; 9.10; 10.27; 14.2, 26-27; 15.16, 33; 16.6; 19.23; 22.4; 24.21; 28.14; 29.25; 31.30). As a result, they are confident (14.26) but also cautious, carefully considering the direction they take (14.15-16; 22.5). They are honest (4.24; 6.16-19; 10.18; 12.19; 14.5, 25; 17.4; 20.10, 23; 24.26, 28; 26.19; 27.6) but do not speak much (10.19; 17.27; 18.21). They are peace-loving, doing everything they can to soothe tension (see comments on Proverbs 16 above) and seldom getting angry (12.16; 14.29; 15.18; 16.32; 19.11; 29.11, 22). But they do not bend reality to avoid confrontation because they are just (1.3; 2.9; 17.23; 18.5; 19.28; 21.3, 15; 22.8; 28.5). They work very hard (6.6-11; 10.5; 12.11; 13.4; 20.4; 24.30-34) and are generous with their goods (11.25; 12.10; 22.9). The image of peaceful, careful, self-controlled people does not mean they are boring or passive. The quest for wisdom is all about passion. Words for emotions are frequent in Proverbs and the way chapters 1–9 compare the student's relationship with wisdom to a young man's relationship with women also suggests that the ideal person is passionate and has strong desires (Yoder 2019:18). But these desires and passions are well directed.

Although this description of the ideal person is gleaned from the text of Proverbs, it is not found there directly. Proverbs uses many negative and positive categories to speak about humans: 'the wise', 'the righteous', 'the fool' and so on. We learn about these characters by seeing them in different situations, but they are never defined explicitly. Millar suggests that this is perhaps because they cannot be defined by a list of exclusive characteristics. The group of wise people is

> analogous to a family, where some characteristics – build, temperament, facial features – may be shared by Granddad Bill and Uncle Charles but not by Great Aunt Eloise. … No single member must exhibit every feature, nor must a single feature be shared by every member. The category's makeup is much more fluid and open.
>
> (Millar 2020:94)

Having said this, there may be some exceptions. For example, according to at least some of the writers of Proverbs, the fear of God should define every wise person (1.7). Also, the wise are often associated with characteristics such as humility (11.2), the ability to listen and accept discipline (10.8; 12.15; 13.1, 10; 15.5, 12, 31; 17.10; 19.25; 21.11) and the ability to produce speech which is healing (12.18; 13.14) rather than harmful (11.12).

Unlike 'the wise' and 'the fool', 'the righteous' and 'the wicked' are seldom described in terms of their characteristics. We read more about the consequences of their conduct ('blessings for the head of the righteous' (10.6a); 'the righteous are delivered from trouble' (11.8a)). However, as the righteous and the wise seem to be co-referential, like the wicked and the fool, the characteristics of the wise and the fool can be applied to the righteous and the wicked, respectively (Keefer 2017:109; Millar 2020:106).

The wise/fool and the righteous/wicked are the most common antithetical pairs, but there are others: diligent/lazy (12.24), rich/poor (13.7), intelligent/scoffer (14.6; 19.25) and so on. Proverbs never speaks about righteous fools. This is not because its writers were hopelessly naive. They were aware that no human being was perfectly pure (20.9). They probably wanted to present ideal prototypes because that is a more effective pedagogical tool than considering mixed characters (for how prototypes work in character formation, see Millar 2020:94–5).

The behaviour of these ideal characters is always in harmony with their knowledge. Michael Fox (2009:934–43) compares this aspect of Proverbs to Socratic ethics, according to which no one would knowingly do wrong and harmful things. To use a simple example, when a person commits adultery, it is not because desire overwrites the knowledge that adultery is wrong. True knowledge cannot be overwritten, so the person has probably never really understood that adultery is wrong. This is why justice has to be understood: 'evil men do not understand justice, but those who seek YHWH understand it all' (28.5; see 1.3; 29.7). In this holistic world view, virtue, the will, knowledge and desire form a unity (Millar 2020:92; see also my notes on the human heart in my comments on 4.20-27 above). Once righteousness is understood, it is also desired.

Therefore, according to Proverbs, stupid people are also evil and good people are wise. Yet the picture is not completely black and white. While there is no clear gradation in good characters, bad characters are not all equally bad. At one end of the spectrum, the evildoer (*rasha*) and scoffer (*lets*) are hopeless. Since they ridicule good teaching, they will never be able to learn (9.7-9; 13.1; 14.7; 15.12; 19.25; 21.11; see Fox 1997:65–7). The fool (*kesil*) is almost as bad. They are simply not interested in wisdom (17.24) because they enjoy doing foolish things (10.23; 14.24). They easily become overconfident (1.32; 28.26) and, consequently, careless and harmful in speech (18.2, 6-7; 19.1). Discipline will affect them little (17.10). Yet they are not completely hopeless (8.5; 26.5, 12; 29.20), though teaching them is a nightmare. A simple person (*peti*) is perhaps the best of the bad bunch (but see the negative portrayal of the simple in Keefer 2017:111), somewhere in the middle between light and darkness, an inexperienced, often young, person who is (still) malleable but prone to gullibility (14.15). Not surprisingly, the simple is the primary target of both Dame Folly and Lady Wisdom in chapters 1–9 (for an excellent discussion of these and many other categories, see Fox 2000:28–43).

Not being overconfident seems to be the secret of being wise (see the many sayings about pride and humility, for example, 3.34; 8.13; 15.33; 11.2; 21.24; 22.4). People obtain wisdom not despite their limitations but because they are aware of them. Scoffers and fools cannot be taught because they think they are knowledgeable. Self-doubt is a virtue. Only God knows what is going on in our darkest chambers ('the life-breath of man is YHWH's lamp, he examines all the chambers of the belly' (20.27); see 15.3, 11).

Epistemology

What is the source of human knowledge? Many think that Proverbs, in contrast to much of the Bible, has an empirical approach.

> While a great deal of wisdom resided beyond human understanding, the 'sages' engaged in persistent efforts to know empirically and rationally the natural and social world that they encountered. ... Most did not lay claim to any special revelation in their speculations.
>
> (Perdue 2008:55; see also Crenshaw 1998a:120–2, 281; Schipper 2019b:32; Goldingay 2019:52, 55; McLaughlin 2019)

> While the prophet announces: 'thus says the Lord,' and the scribe argues: 'it is written,' the wise says: 'I have observed.'
>
> (Steinberg 2019:186)

The lazy person is encouraged to study the ant and learn diligence from it (6.6-11). The wisdom teacher bases his lessons on what he sees through his window (7.6-7). He investigates the sad state of a vineyard and draws conclusions about the detrimental effects of procrastination (24.30-34). The list could go on. The book is teeming with observations apparently from the careful, empirical study of the natural world and human nature (for example, 'Anxiety weighs down the human heart, but a good word cheers it up' (12.25)). Some interpreters go as far as to claim that the authors of Proverbs 'were the first psychologists and sociologists as well as ethicists and philosophers' (Sneed 2015a:241) and that 'today, the human sciences can be seen as a prolongation of the ancient wisdom approach' (Steinberg 2019:197; similarly, Birch et al. 2005:383).

Some have argued that modern natural theology is also a prolongation of the wisdom approach (Barr 1993:173; Brueggemann 1996:178; VanDrunen 2013). Accordingly, the book's authors observed nature and drew conclusions from it about the relationship between God and humans.

A form of theological thought was established that is fundamental to Proverbs 10–22: a 'natural theology' based on experience that seeks to make general statements about human existence in the world and before God.

(Schipper 2019a:357; see also 33–4)

But clearly not all of Proverbs is rooted in the empirical investigation of the world. It notes the limitations of human observation (14.12; 16.2, 25; 20.12, 24; 21.2) and refers to YHWH (1.7; 29.18; 30.5-6) or to parental teaching (that is, tradition; 1.8; 2.1 and so on) as authorities. Consequently, Barr argues (1993:147), the natural theology of Proverbs is poorly done. Others are more appreciative of the writers' attempts to keep empirical studies and revealed religion together. Millar, for example, thinks that Proverbs validates both listening to instruction and personal observation. Revelation provides a framework which directs our investigation of the world, but what we experience also influences our understanding of revelation (2020:193). Schipper sees a historical movement from observation, through recognition of limitations, to revelation in the sapiential tradition.

The key point for understanding the book of Proverbs is that this theology based on human experience was increasingly questioned. ... Human perception itself reveals the limits of a concept of wisdom that seeks to derive abstract knowledge from empirical observation.

(Schipper 2021:34; see also
Crenshaw 1998a:211, 250, 252, 258)

As a result of this chronological development, the received form of the book contains both approaches:

[The YHWH sayings] often occur alongside sayings emphasizing practical experience. ... The coexistence of alternative positions results in a synthesis that could be described as 'discursive linking.' The ... different positions ... stand alongside each other, allowing for a critical discourse on the benefits and limits of sapiential knowledge.

(Schipper 2019a:36)

However, not everyone sees empiricism in Proverbs. When it directs our attention to nature, it tells us what to find there, which is hardly an empirical approach. In 6.6-11 it does not say 'Observe the ant', but 'Observe the ant; see that it does not have a ruler, yet, it is industrious' (which, by the way, is not completely true (Schipper 2019a:226)). Nothing in the text suggests that the teacher has ever studied ants. It is just an illustrative story (Fox 2007:672–3). When the father explains in 7.6-7 what he saw through his window, he does not base his teaching on it. It is a story (heavily interpreted by the teacher (Schipper 2019a:252–81)) that illustrates the teaching of the previous chapters. Even when the teacher claims to have arrived at a conclusion following an observation (24.30-34), it is more 'an illustrative story, not an account of a new philosophical insight' (Weeks 2012:143). The sayings that describe the world (for example, 12.25) do not state whether the information is drawn from experience or revelation. They never encourage readers to observe things. Quite the opposite, they provide a lens through which to view experience. As Michael V. Fox (2007, 2009b:967–76) explains, Proverbs uses a 'coherence theory' of knowledge. Truth is validated not by experiential data but by agreement with the book's system of compatible beliefs (see also Sandoval 2006:6–10, 64–6; Viljoen and Venter 2013).

Perhaps Proverbs does not teach empiricism but, argue some scholars, neither does it teach revelation (Miller 2015:105). Annette Schellenberg (2015:126–30) adds that wisdom literature never refers to any human mediators of revelation. If revelation is available, it is available to everyone or at least to the educated elite and not only to one or two selected people.

Therefore, there is a lively debate. Some maintain that Proverbs promotes empiricism. Some think it validates both empiricism and revelation. Some think it lacks empiricism but presupposes tradition and revelation. Finally, some think that it does not promote revelation, at least not the kind of revelation that is given through a special person.

Amidst this storm of scholarly debate, is it possible to name the key characteristics of Proverbs' epistemology that most scholars would agree on? Let me try to suggest three such characteristics. First, empirically or not, Proverbs encourages its readers to look below the surface. Whether this happens through human investigation of the world or with divine help, we should solve riddles (1.6), see through misleading behaviour (28.11) and anticipate unexpected outcomes (14.8, 15). This investigative spirit does not contradict Deuteronomy 29.29 ('The secret things belong to the LORD our God, but the revealed things belong to us' (NRSV)), but it changes the emphasis.

Second, even if references to human experiences are 'illustrative stories', they are still important. Adam R. Shapiro notes how natural images have often been used in post-biblical natural theology, not to build logical arguments but to involve all the senses and imagination of the reader in the project of understanding. Natural theologians showed an understanding of how humans think: ... of how nature and divinity can open one's mind and spirit to be moved and persuaded. ... This says much about the long tradition of natural theology as an engagement of embodiment and emotion, through touching, feeling and *sensing*. ... This synthesis of knowledge as both thinking and sensing was key to the emergence of empiricism.

(Shapiro 2022, emphasis in original)

Descriptions of the created world in Proverbs qualify as 'natural theology', at least in this limited, rhetorical sense. They engage the whole human being, whose understanding requires more than proofs (though, in this respect, Proverbs is no different from other parts of the Bible).

Third, related to engaging all the senses, Crenshaw's insight about the erotic nature of knowledge should also be noted.

The fascination with erotic language in regard to wisdom cannot simply be explained as teachers' attempts to capture the interest of young boys. The endless quest for knowledge, the excitement over discovering new insights, the seductive lure and secretive hiding of truth – all this resembles an amorous adventure where lovers come together and bask in each other's arms.

(Crenshaw 1998a:202; see also pp. 70, 179; Brown 2019:74; O'Dowd 2009:119; Forti 2020:185–6; Schellenberg 2018:257)

Wisdom is sexy!

Selected works

Chapters 1–9

Historical and social background of Proverbs 1–9
Dell 2006, 2009, 2016; Schweitzer 2012; Shupak 2011; Yoder 2001

Structure and redactional history of Proverbs 1–9
Keefer 2020; Pemberton 2005; Schipper 2021; Wendland 2020; Zabán 2012

Women in Proverbs
Aletti 1977; Blenkinsopp 1991; Camp 2000; Estes 2010; Fischer 2019; Forti 2007, 2020; Goff 2015; Maier 2014; Shupak 2011; Tan Nam Hoon 2008; Yoder 2001. Yee (1989) argues that the speeches of women form a chiastic structure. An excellent bibliography on Lady Wisdom can be found in Bledsoe 2013:121–2, notes 5–7.

Ethics and theology of Proverbs 1–9
Baris 2015; Estes 1997

Overview
Most of these issues are discussed in Weeks 2007.

Chapters 10–31

Mashal
Vayntrub 2019:36–69

Literary form, poetic imagery
Luchsinger 2010; Rotasperti 2021; Stewart 2016:29–69; Williams 1995

Genre studies (definition, diversity and significance)
Millar 2022; Sneed 2015a:183–215; Weeks 2015

Paremiology
For a general introduction, see Hrisztova-Gotthardt and Varga 2014; for paremiology and biblical proverbs, see Nahkola 2016 and Seal 2021.

Openness of sayings
Kselman 2002; Millar 2020; Miller 2003; Noegel 2021

World view of Proverbs

(Creation) theology (including world order, act–consequence relationships, reward and retribution)
Boström 1990; Dell 2022, 2023; Fox 1995; van Leeuwen 2021; Perdue 1994; Schwáb 2022a; Zimmerli 1964

The world view of Proverbs versus the rest of the Hebrew Bible
Dell 2006; Weeks 2016; Zimmerli 1964

Epistemology
Fox 2007; Schellenberg 2015

Character types, character formation, pedagogy
Brown 2022; Fox 1997; Keefer 2022; Millar 2020:89–110; Stewart 2016; Yoder 2005

Part III

The biblical context

Wisdom literature

For much of the twentieth century, the scholarly consensus was that Proverbs, Job and Ecclesiastes (with perhaps some parts of other books) comprised the 'wisdom literature', a part of the Bible that shows little interest in the election of Israel, divine revelation and salvation history. The uniqueness of wisdom literature was explained by its unique authorship. It was written by a special group, the sages, who were trained in special schools and who were indifferent or even opposed to the views of the other biblical writers, the priests and prophets. These highly educated, cosmopolitan sages were enculturated in international literature, culture and politics. They were mainly interested in the empirically recognizable world order and in how it could be used to lead a successful life. Proverbs represented their classic teaching, while Job and Ecclesiastes were written when they realized that a rigid understanding of world order simply did not fit real life (Crenshaw 1998a:146). The world view of wisdom literature, which focused on creation and individuals, represented an alternative tradition to other biblical books, which focused on the nation and history (a classic statement of this old scholarly consensus is found in Crenshaw 1976).

Each element of this old consensus is up for debate today. The reasons are many. First, the central tenet of form criticism on which the old consensus depended has been questioned. Form criticism teaches that different literary forms are the products of different life settings (*Sitze im Leben*). However, it is now acknowledged that people in different life settings can produce similar texts, or the same group of people can write in different styles (Dell and Kynes 2019:1–2; Weeks 2015:164–7; for Egyptian 'wisdom authors' producing 'non-wisdom' books, see Fox 2015b:72–3). Therefore, any direct correspondence between 'wisdom literature' and a well-defined group of sages is difficult to establish. Second, recent historical research suggests that the same scribal culture was responsible for creating the whole Hebrew Bible, not only the wisdom literature (see discussion in Part I). This again suggests that a group of internationally minded sages (as opposed to nationalistic priests and prophets) may not have existed. Third, the category of 'wisdom literature' is a modern, nineteenth-century scholarly invention (Kynes 2019a:82–104). The three biblical books which supposedly comprise it (Proverbs, Ecclesiastes, Job) are as different from each other as they are from other biblical books (Weeks 2015:174).

Some scholars have suggested that 'wisdom literature' is a genre. It is not the world view of 'wisdom texts' that is distinctive but their mode of expression. This approach solves some problems but raises other tricky questions. What is the definition of a genre? How do different genres interact, especially if detected within a single text? Are there (sub)genres within genres? How should the recognition of genres influence interpretation? (For these and other genre-related questions, see Dell 2020:22–4; Fox 2015b:75–83; Kynes 2019a:107–45; Sneed 2015a:183–215; Weeks 2015.)

Kynes (2019a) suggests that it would be better to stop using the 'wisdom literature' label altogether or at least admit its heuristic nature. Depending on the focus, the biblical books can be arranged in different ways. If we concentrate on poetic forms, the Song of Songs is closer to Proverbs than Ecclesiastes. If we focus on the concept of wisdom, then Ecclesiastes is closer to Proverbs than the Song of Songs, but 1 Kings 1–11 is even closer. Our question determines which biblical books we associate with Proverbs.

Not everyone is ready to relinquish the category of 'wisdom literature'. Fox notes that although literary categories are scholarly constructs, this is no reason to abandon them. Shellenberg notes that even if all the biblical books were produced by a group of scribes, there may have been subgroups with distinct interests contributing to different parts of the Bible. Dell compares 'wisdom literature' to a family. She borrows the image of the family from Wittgenstein, thus getting around the difficulty of defining common denominators in the wisdom books. For example, most members of a family may be blond, but not everyone, while there are many blond people outside the family too. No family can claim exclusive possession of any characteristic. Furthermore, all human beings are related, just as all the books of the Bible are connected, but it would be ridiculous to argue that there are no such things as families. These and many rival opinions are conveniently collected in WTWT.

Questioning the category of 'wisdom literature' need not have led to abandoning it completely but has created a milieu in which scholars are more willing to recognize similarities and dialogue between Proverbs and other biblical books outside 'wisdom literature'. I will briefly highlight some examples.

Intertextuality and canonical criticism

Intertextuality investigates how texts are related and how these relationships modify interpretation. Canonical criticism investigates similar questions within the boundary of a canon. In this chapter all my examples are from the Hebrew Bible, although intertextual readings between Proverbs and other texts have also been undertaken.

Genesis

Biblical characters often seem to embody some aspects of the teaching in Proverbs. Interpreters wonder whether some parts of Proverbs may have inspired biblical stories or vice versa. Several characters in Genesis (Abraham, Jacob, Tamar, Judah and Joseph) have been understood by certain interpreters as portraying proverbial wisdom or folly (Harris 1995; Ska 2014; Sneed 2011; von Rad 1966b). These suggestions are interesting but not accepted by everyone (for the debate about Joseph, see Weeks 1999:92–109; Wilson 2004).

The connection between Proverbs 8.22-31 and Genesis 1 is less controversial. Both speak of creation as a past event (whereas most biblical references depict it as God's ongoing activity: see Ps. 104; Prov. 16.4; 17.5; 20.12; 22.2; see Dell 2010:65). Both passages mention the 'beginning' (Gen. 1.1; Prov. 8.22) and only these two texts in the Hebrew Bible use the phrase 'on the surface of the deep' (Gen. 1.2a; Prov. 8.22b). Reading the two passages together suggests an identification between the wind/spirit of God and Wisdom (Gen. 1.2; Prov. 8.22; Bauks and Baumann 1994:49–50; see also Prov. 3.19-20 and Ps. 104.24, which state that God created the universe 'by wisdom'). This explains why post-biblical Christian tradition has identified the wisdom of Proverbs 8 with the Holy Spirit and with Christ himself (see Yoder 2021:273, 278; Ticciati 2021).

Perhaps the clearest intertextual connection with Genesis, however, is with the Eden story. In the entire Hebrew Bible, only Genesis and Proverbs mention the tree of life. Christine Roy Yoder (2019) argues that the context of Proverbs 3.18a ('She [Wisdom] is a tree of life for those who grasp her') confirms that it is a deliberate reference to Genesis 2.9 and 3.22 (see also Hurowitz 2004). This is suggested by the Eden motifs in Proverbs 3.13-20: waters (3.20; see Gen. 2.5 and 2.10-14), gold and jewels (3.14-15; see Gen. 2.10-14), desire (3.15; see desirable trees and Eve's desire in Gen. 2.9; 3.6) and peace and tranquillity (3.17; see life in Eden before pain, toil and sweat are announced in Gen. 3.16-19). Yoder concludes that 3.18 teaches that 'wisdom is the tree of life. The forbidden tree is forbidden no longer' (2019:12). The theological implication of this teaching is that

> wisdom ... restores what was lost long ago, namely, a flourishing life in Eden. ... At the same time, the poem in its immediate literary setting resists any notion that that restoration to the garden is also to a naïve, idyllic existence apart from the world. ... The peace of wisdom's paths is not ... removed from and immune to everyday complexities and challenges. Instead, the great fortune (vv. 13, 18) of those who find and grab onto wisdom, the tree of life, is flourishing and joy in the thick of it all.
>
> (Yoder 2019:18)

Yoder's claim that 'wisdom is the tree of life' may be a slight overstatement. In 3.18 wisdom is 'a tree of life', not 'the tree of life'. Therefore, they are not identical. Nonetheless, wisdom is the best functional equivalent of the tree of life available to us, as it provides life, just like the tree of life in the Garden of Eden.

More importantly, I suggest extending Yoder's argument to other elements of Proverbs 1-9. Just as Adam and Eve had a choice between two similar trees, the tree of life and the tree of the knowledge of good and evil, so Proverbs presents a choice between wisdom that gives life and something that looks like wisdom but leads to death. This choice becomes particularly obvious in chapter 9, where two women, Lady Wisdom and Dame Folly, issue invitations. Both have a house in a high place (9.1, 14), use similar words inviting 'the simple ones' (9.4, 16) and offer a prepared table (9.2-5, 15-17). But these similarities mask a fundamental difference. The food of one leads to life (9.6) and the food of the other to death (9.18), like Eden's two trees. The people invited, the 'simple ones', also remind us of Genesis

2–3. The simple ones are inexperienced and without knowledge, just like Adam and Eve (Clines 1974:9). Thus, in Proverbs 9, as in Genesis 3, simple people are faced with a choice between two kinds of food, the food of death (folly) and the food of life (wisdom).

Later verses in Proverbs that mention the tree of life can also be brought into the argument. Yoder resists this because they are 'individual proverbs which … confound much intertextual analysis' (2019:11–12). But I think she gives up on them too easily. The verses following 13.12 speak about despising commandments (13.13) and life and death (13.14), which can remind the reader how Adam and Eve disregarded God's commandment, thereby losing life and gaining death. (Michaela Bauks (2015:24–6) also highlights a number of verbal parallels between Genesis 3 and Proverbs 13.12-19.)

> [12] A frustrated hope is sickness for the heart, but a fulfilled desire is a **tree of life**. [13] The one who despises the word will be destroyed, but the one fearing the **commandment** will be well. [14] The teaching of wisdom is a fountain of **life** for avoiding snares of **death**.

Proverbs 15:4 is immediately preceded by the words 'evil' and 'good', again reminding us of the story about the knowledge of good and evil.

> [3] The eyes of the Lord are everywhere, watching the **evil** and the **good**. [4] The healing tongue is a **tree of life**, but crookedness in it breaks the spirit.

These echoes of Eden motifs may be accidental. They are barely enough to call to mind the story of Adam and Eve. But if Genesis 3 is already in the mind of the reader, Proverbs 13.12-14 and 15.3-4 can easily be understood as everyday applications of it: listening to commandments (13.12-14) is like eating from the tree of life and speaking truthfully but graciously (15.4-5) is like giving the fruit of the tree of life to others.

The remaining verse, Proverbs 11.30, is puzzling: 'the fruit of the righteous is a tree of life and the wise takes lives away'. Why would the wise take lives away? A possible solution is to amend the Hebrew by changing the word for 'wise' to a similar word which means 'violence' (Osborne 2020:107–8). However, there is another possibility (Fox 2009:545). We can understand *laqah* ('take away') in *colon* B not as 'kill' but as 'save' (that is, take away from danger), or perhaps as 'captivate' (that is, the teaching of the wise attracts people). Accordingly, the righteous (11.30a) and the wise (11.30b) are associated and their fruit (always a metaphor for speech in 10.1–22.16; see 12.14; 13.2; 18.20-21) produces life in others, like the fruit of the tree of life.

All the individual sentences in Proverbs 10.1-22.16 that mention the tree of life can be understood as relating to speech. Listening to (wise) commandments is like eating that mythical, life-giving fruit and speaking wisely is like giving that fruit to others. This is not surprising, since wisdom which is manifested in wise speech is like a tree of life, as we learn in 3.18.

Deuteronomy

The many parallels between Proverbs and Deuteronomy are unmistakable:

> Deuteronomy reverberates throughout Proverbs 3, in the emphasis on choosing life (3:8; cf. Deut 4:40; 5:16; 11:9, 21), the mention of offering first fruits (3:9; cf. Deut 14:22–29; 26:1–2), and allusions to the Shema (e.g., Prov 3:3, 5; Deut 6:4–9) …, which recur in Prov 6:20–24 and 7:1–5 …. Further 'echoes' of Deuteronomy also ring out across the rest of Proverbs [for instance]. … the falsification of weights (Deut 25:13–16; cf. Prov 11:1; 20:23), moving property boundaries (Deut 19:14; cf. Prov 22:28; 23:10), treatment of slaves (Deut 23:16; cf. Prov 30:10), partiality in judgement (Deut 1:17; cf. Prov 24:23), and pursuit of righteousness (Deut 16:20; cf. Prov 21:21) …. The repeated references to *torah* in 28:4–9 suggest a broader Deuteronomic background to the Hezekian collection (Prov 25:1–29:27 …), and allusions to Deuteronomy also appear in the Words of Agur in Proverbs 30 (e.g., Prov 30:6; cf. Deut 4:2; 13:1 [ET 12:32] …).
>
> (Kynes 2019b:39; for more detailed comparison
> see Schipper 2021; Weinfeld 1972)

The intertextual relationship of Proverbs and Deuteronomy has been discussed very often. However, throughout the twentieth century and up until now, many have argued against a direct literary relationship. Social transgressions such as removing boundary markers and using false measures were condemned throughout the ancient Near East, so the occurrence of such ideas in two biblical books does not imply a relationship. Words like 'torah' or 'commandments' may refer to the divine laws in Deuteronomy and to the parental teachings in Proverbs without implying any connection between them (for such views, see Clifford 1999:5, 243–4; Fishbane 1985:288; Fox 2000:79, 2009b:951–3; *WTWT*:304).

The most influential challenge to this opinion came from Moshe Weinfeld, who argued that the authors of Deuteronomy were scribes influenced by the kind of wisdom we find in Proverbs 10–29 (1972:244–81). Weinfeld has not persuaded everyone. Many have pointed out that his concept of 'wisdom circles' is ill-defined, that similarities can often be explained by the common usage of language in the seventh and sixth centuries BCE, and that Proverbs and Deuteronomy contain as many significant differences as similarities (Crenshaw 1998a:233–4; Fox 2009:951–3; Rofé 2002:220–5). Schniedewind's response is that differences do not prove anything, as ancient scribes usually adapted their proverbs to different situations (2019:140).

This ongoing debate is illustrated by different interpretations of Proverbs 3.3, 5 and 6.21 and Deuteronomy 6.4-9. Fox (2000:144–9, 228–9) interprets the verses in Proverbs without any significant reference to Deuteronomy. Carr (2011:418–19) argues that the authors of Deuteronomy were influenced by the text of Proverbs. Schipper (2019a:125, 237) thinks that Deuteronomy influenced Proverbs 3 and 6.

Schipper's theory is particularly noteworthy. In his view, the relationship between Proverbs and Deuteronomy is more complex than previously assumed. Both Deuteronomy and Proverbs are the results of editorial activity over a long period of time, during which the development of the two books overlapped, so each influenced the writing of the other. As a result, the relationship between Deuteronomy and Proverbs keeps changing. For example, Proverbs 2 argues that wisdom helps people understand the (deuteronomistic) Torah, Proverbs 6 presents wisdom as the Torah itself, while Proverbs 3 and 30 emphasize the limitations of wisdom compared to the Torah (2019b, 2021).

These debates affect the interpretation of Proverbs greatly. If, for example, Schipper is right that Proverbs 2 deliberately alludes to Deuteronomy, it explains why 2.22 refers to the wicked as cut off from the land – the sentiment of Deuteronomy 28. Also, if at least some parts of Proverbs reflect on Deuteronomy, wisdom was not considered quite as separate from other religious traditions as many have thought. On the contrary, 'full convergence between *lex* [law] and *sapientia* [wisdom] can be found *in*, rather than *beyond*, Proverbs' (Brown 2005:278). If, however, Fox, Crenshaw and Clifford are right and the authors of Proverbs did not reflect on Deuteronomy, it is perfectly legitimate to seek the meaning of proverbial language on its own, even if it looks familiar from Deuteronomy.

It seems to me that one limitation of most of the Deuteronomy-related debates is that they focus on the historical question of which text influenced which. This is important, but it tends to overshadow the question of how one text can be read in the light of the other, regardless of any direct literary relationship. My suspicion is that a canonical reading that builds on the parallels between Deuteronomy and Proverbs could offer deep theological reflections on the relationship between (human) wisdom and the deuteronomistic Torah, even if we reserve judgement about the order or existence of a literary relationship.

Selected works

Wisdom literature

Kynes (2019a) abandons the category. Various views are expressed in *WTWT*.

Intertextuality and canonical criticism

For the concepts of canonical criticism and intertextuality, see Dell and Kynes 2019; Grohmann and Kim 2019 and Scheetz 2011:1–35.

Dell and Kynes (2013); O'Dowd (2019) and Sandoval (2019, 2020a) discuss many intertextual connections.

Genesis and Proverbs

For the relationship between Proverbs and Genesis 1–3, see Yoder 2001. Bauks and Baumann 1994 and Bauks 2015 (in German) provide more detailed exegetical analysis.

Deuteronomy and Proverbs

Classic works: Weinfeld 1972 and Rofé 2002. Fox (2009:951–3) provides a summary and critique of Weinfeld 1972. More recently Schipper (2019b, 2021) discussed the relationship between Proverbs and Deuteronomy. Like Schipper, Heckl (2015) and Weeks (2007) also think that the word 'torah' can have a similar meaning in Proverbs 1–9 and in Deuteronomy.

Part IV

The context of the reader

Part IV is of necessity very selective. There are many ideological approaches to Proverbs: queer (Stuart 2006), disability (Melcher 2017), ecological (Dell 2010; Wurst 2001) and so on. I will make a few comments only on three: feminist, African and theological interpretations, with a special emphasis on the middle one because it is still under-represented in the literature on Proverbs.

Feminist interpretation

In Proverbs we read about a mother (1.8; 4.3; 6.20; 10.1; 15.20; 19.26; 20.20; 23.22-25; 28.24; 29.15; 30.11, 17); Lady Wisdom (1.20-33; 3.11-20; 8; 9.1-6); a strange woman (2.16-19; 5; 6.20-35; 7); the wife of a son (5.15-19); Dame Folly (9.13-18); gracious, beautiful, stupid, wise and destructive women (11.16, 22; 14.1; 31.3); a good wife (12.4; 18.22; 19.14); a nagging wife (19.13; 21:9, 19; 25:24; 27:15); an adulterous wife (30.20); the girl (30.19); an unloved woman (30.23); a queen mother (31.1); and a capable woman (31.10-31).

Obviously, women are prime subjects of the book. Not surprisingly, the book is therefore a prime subject of feminist biblical interpretation. Some interpreters celebrate how feminine language is (re)introduced into speech about divinity through the divine figure of Lady Wisdom and how the capable woman is presented as a strong, assertive female character with initiative. They also argue that the book has the potential to renew theological thinking in general. After all, Proverbs' wisdom is local and relational; no one can fully possess it; it is reflected in human experience; and it connects emotions, desires and cognition holistically. All these challenge the long tradition of oppressive, patriarchal systems of knowledge (Claassens 2016; Fentress-Williams and Knowles 2018; Yoder 2021).

At the same time, Proverbs has a strong gender bias which is often critically exposed by feminist interpreters. They point out how the figure of the strange woman lacks genuine human motivation. We do not read about her emotional, financial and physical needs. Any trace of vulnerability is missing from her character. She is depicted as the quintessential 'other', who, like an evil demon, hunts innocent boys. The father, it is argued, is threatened by female sexuality, so he tries to control it (Camp 2000:40–89; Yee 2003:135–58).

Even the positive female figures fail to impress everyone. The celebration of idealized, perfect, perhaps divine women easily diverts attention away from the real sufferings of real women. As Fontaine writes,

> the elevated female figures, such as Lady Wisdom (Prov. 1–9) or the Strong Woman (Prov. 31.10-31), may be inversely proportional to the 'truth' of real women's lives. That is, such fine figures may just as easily be an index of women's lack of power and status, a drugged sop thrown to a beaten dog.
>
> (Fontaine 2002:15)

Although Lady Wisdom and the capable woman can be paraded as paragons of positive values, all real women fall short of such semi-divine icons and this may be a motive to oppress them.

The fundamental problem is that Proverbs' discussion of women (and anything else) reveals its hierarchical, patriarchal perspective (for an eco-feminist criticism of this, see Hobgood-Oster 2001). Women are discussed not because they are appreciated in themselves but because a father is speaking to a son whose object of desire happens to be women. Daughters who would like to seek wisdom are excluded from the audience. Women are valued because of what they can give to men. These women are either absolutely good or absolutely bad, depending on the men's perspective (Claassens 2016; Dell 2006:86; Masenya 2018b:4; Sneed 2015a:293–5).

Of course, many of these points are debated. In his response to feminist critiques of Proverbs, Fox argues that the woman is not the quintessential 'other' in Proverbs, as this is the 'evildoer' and the father is not threatened by female sexuality – he simply condemns adultery. Nonetheless, Fox acknowledges that Proverbs is androcentric because it never addresses women (Fox 2000:256–62).

African interpretation

My account of the African interpretation of Proverbs can be summarized in seven points:

1 It often starts by noting similarities between ancient Israelite and African societies.
2 It seeks the transformation of society.
3 It focuses on three key issues: comparison with African proverbs, poverty and the situation of women.
4 It is embedded in the analysis of African society.
5 It focuses on local issues.
6 It is diverse.
7 It recognizes the responsibility of the interpreter and often reflects on hermeneutical questions.

In the following I elaborate on each point.

Similarities between ancient Israelite and African societies

African interpretations often start by noting similarities between ancient Israelites and Africans. Agrarian life and strict work ethics characterize many people in both societies (Kimilike 2018:138–41; Masenya 2015:423). African tribes have taboos and rites separating them from others, just like the ancient Israelites had food taboos and the rite of circumcision (Kimilike 2018:138–41). Many African tribal religions believe in one creator God (Kimilike 2018:140). Just as we have seen in Proverbs, African culture is family-oriented, assigning the responsibility of education to parents (Masenya 2020:473–4). The primary aim of education is character development, as character-based African ethics teach that 'it is from a person's character that all his or her actions – good or bad – radiate' (Ademiluka 2018:175; see also Kimilike 2018:138–41; for similar views in Proverbs, see Brown 1996, 2014). The African world view, just like that of Proverbs, has an 'optimistic outlook' on life that emphasizes material rewards for hard work (Masenya 2015:428, 2020:471). The African 'holistic world-view' sees material and spiritual well-being as a unity (compare Proverbs' emphasis on long life and wealth)

(Nel 2012:464). African fables and stories borrow images from nature (Masenya 2015:422). Many African proverbs portray women as extremely industrious household managers, similarly to Proverbs 31.10-31 (Masenya 2016:367, 2018a).

African scholars, Kimilike (2008, 2018) argues, can see aspects of Proverbs that may be invisible to Western scholars. As one interesting example, he observes how Western interpreters understand 'Give beer to those who are perishing' in Proverbs 31.6-7 as cynical advice. In Bena (Tanzania) culture, however, drinking beer is an important communal activity, through which people come together, discuss action and share efforts. Seeing the proverb through this cultural lens, it is not promoting numbing the senses but quite the opposite: King Lemuel is encouraged to empower the poor so that they can fight for their rights (2018:147–8, 154–6).

Ademiluke (2018) regrets the gradual loss of African values among young people, seeing this as one of causes of social disintegration and poverty. He thinks that teaching Proverbs in schools could reawaken elements of the traditional African value system, such as respect for parents or feeling shame when getting rich by unethical means.

Others use the similarities between African life and Proverbs to highlight structures of oppression. Masenya (2018a), for instance, remarks that the husband of the capable woman, like many African men, enjoys the social prestige and political power provided by his wife's hard work. She adds that African women are even more disadvantaged than the capable woman, as they lack her financial power.

In general, such parallels enable African scholars to free themselves from European, Western ideological dominance and claim Proverbs as their home territory. After all, parts of Proverbs may have been borrowed or copied from Africa (see 22.17–24.22 and its similarities to the Egyptian *Instructions of Amenemope*; Ramantswana 2017:365), so it is time for Africa to take Proverbs back. Ordinary Africans can also take back interpreting Proverbs from experts who often represent European, Western ideological dominance (Kimilike 2018:135).

Transforming society

While much of Western interpretation emphasizes understanding the text in the ancient world of its origin (Nel 2012:462), many African interpreters see in this a 'complicity of western elitist avoidance'. Western scholars fail to prove 'the practicality of their biblical interpretation' (Kimilike 2018:144).

African interpretation seeks to transform twenty-first-century African society by recognizing the biblical resources for rooting out injustice (Kimilike 2018:136, 142; see also Nel 2012:465).

African proverbs, poverty and women

African proverbs

Proverbs are a vital part of African life (van Heerden 2002:462; Masenya 2020:465). They convey difficult messages without offending ('Proverbs are the palm-oil with which words are eaten'; Igbo proverb, Nigeria); they guide conversations ('A proverb is the horse which carries a subject under discussion along; if a subject under discussion goes astray, we use a proverb to track it'; Yoruba saying, Nigeria) (Ademiluka 2018:176; Antwi, Adjei and Asuming 2020:418). They instil values (Ademiluka 2018:176; Chebet and Cherop 2015:207) and through their metaphors expose familiar patterns of life ('When beer enters, the brain moves out'; Bena proverb (Tanzania) – not only used about beer but about all kinds of intoxicating things, from status through possessions to knowledge; Kimilike 2018:153).

Westermann (1995) and Golka (1993) investigated the similarities between African and biblical proverbs, but it seems that African proverbs are even closer to biblical proverbs than Westermann and Golka realized. They not only speak about work ethics, character-formation, prudence and sociability but include religiosity. Compare, for example, the following proverbs (all examples are taken from Kimilike 2002:259–60):

The rich and the poor meet together, the Lord is the Maker of them all. (Prov. 22.2)	God created the rich and the poor. (Asante, Fante, Aniocha, Igbo proverb)
The eyes of the Lord are every place, keeping watch on the evil and the good. (Prov. 15.3)	Do not count on the fact that you are alone in a quiet spot, for God is above your head. (Malagasy)
The one who is kind to the poor lends to Yahweh and he will reward him for what he has done. (Prov. 19.17)	The person who gives to the poor receives reward from God. (Oromo)

The Akan proverb, 'We are going to consult the old lady,' even personifies wisdom as a woman (Antwi et al. 2020:417, 422).

Not surprisingly, virtually all African interpretations of Proverbs draw on African proverbs, highlighting similarities and occasional differences

(Ramantswana 2017:361–63), in order to shed light on the meaning, social context and use of Israelite proverbs (Adamo 2015). For instance, the contradiction in Proverbs 26.4-5 is less puzzling once we take into account the apparently contradictory African proverbs, 'The hare says, "Walking slowly leads to death." The chameleon says, "Walking quickly leads to death"' (Ewe proverb, van Heerden 2006:437). The use of African proverbs is so pervasive that even interpreters who want to emphasize biblical authority over African cultural products find it virtually impossible to avoid using African proverbs in their arguments (see Biri 2016:230, 234; Davis 2022:181).

Akoto-Abutiate (2014) suggests that because the African tree of life (that is, the wisdom of African proverbs) is so similar to Proverbs' tree of life (that is, the wisdom of Proverbs), it is easy to graft branches of the biblical tree onto the African tree. In other words, it is easy to read biblical proverbs alongside African proverbs, using one to explain the other. She suggests this provides a great opportunity for churches to use the biblical book in their teaching. The image of grafting can also serve as an indigenous metaphor instead of non-African technical terms such as 'inculturation'. The fruit produced by the hybrid tree will be similar but not identical to the fruits of either parent tree.

Poverty

Many, if not most African interpreters of Proverbs, use it to promote the eradication of poverty (Kimilike 2008, 2018 are prime academic examples).

In this respect, Tamie Davis offers an interesting analysis of Ofoo Kassa George's *Biblia Na Utajiri* (The Bible and Wealth). George's is not an academic commentary but a popular work on how to accumulate wealth in a God-fearing way. Western readers may be embarrassed by the promotion of material wealth in Proverbs, but from the African perspective, it makes perfect sense. George uses Proverbs (and other biblical material) to debunk some myths that in her view paralyse African societies:

- That it is fine to pursue wealth at the expense of righteousness
- That you do not need to toil and should just wait for God to make you wealthy
- That it is impossible both to be wealthy and to care for those for whom you are responsible
- That getting rich happens by luck

- That only getting into heaven matters, and pursuing wealth is not a worthy Christian pursuit, and
- That the opportunities for wealth creation are few.

> Ufoo's audience is those who find themselves in situations that are intolerable. … Implicit is the background of poverty in Tanzania and the widely held belief that wealth creation is good because it lifts people out of this situation.
>
> (Davis 2022:179–80)

Seeing Proverbs in the light of these concerns may make its promise of riches more palatable to Western readers, too.

Women

Proverbs 31.10-31 may be the most discussed part of the book in African academic works (see, for example, Biri 2016; Nwaoru 2005), partly because African women recognize aspects of their own lives in the description of the industrious woman (Davis 2019:336) and also because it is frequently used and misused in Africa to justify certain views on gender roles. (But the role of women in other parts of Proverbs is not neglected either; see Masenya 2018b; Olojede 2012.) Some see an assertive woman who can be inspiration to African women, while others emphasize the patriarchal perspective of the passage and use it to point to similar power structures in Africa (Masenya 2016, 2018a, 2020).

Chebet and Cherop (2015) offer an ingenious interpretation. They argue that Proverbs 31.1-9 is a warning against both women and alcohol, the typical temptations that often make African men exploit their wives. Through the lenses of African female experience, the advice of Lemuel's mother (31.1-9), along with the praise of the capable woman (31.10-31), evokes a painfully familiar image: the husband of the capable woman sits idly in the gate (31.23), like many African men who are defeated by their loss of self-control concerning alcohol and women.

Analysis of African society

Almost all African interpretations of Proverbs offer a relatively detailed socio-political analysis of the relevant issues. Whether the use of proverbs, poverty, the meaning of the fear of God or gender roles are examined, readers can expect at least some discussion of African society at a level that would be unusual in European biblical exegesis. Examples include Akoto-Abutiate (2014:12), Biri (2016), Cezula (2017), Chebet and Cherop (2015:193–9), but almost all the works mentioned in this section on African interpretation could be added to the list.

Focus on the local

Although, for the sake of simplicity, I have repeatedly referred broadly to 'African interpretation' or 'African proverbs', most works focus on a specific African context. For instance, there are readings of Proverbs in relation to Sotho/Pedi (South Africa; Masenya 2015, 2018b), Bena (Bantu, Tanzania; Kimilike 2018), Eve (Ghana; Akoto-Abutiate 2014) or Igbo proverbs (south-eastern Nigeria; Ademiluka 2018), to the culture of the Shona people (Bantu, Zimbabwe; Biri 2016), or to typical gender roles in Kenya (Chebet and Cherop 2015). Much of their content may apply to the whole of Africa due to the underlying general traits of many African societies (Masenya 2020:466), but one should not neglect the diversity of African experience reflected in African scholarship.

A striking example of an article that focuses on a specific issue in a given country is Masenya 2017. Masenya compares the strange woman in Proverbs 7 to the recent South African phenomenon of 'sugar mummies' or 'blessers', who reward the sexual services of young men with financial support. She notes the many similarities: affluent married women with absent husbands are sexually involved with inexperienced young men. She remarks on the use of religious language both by the biblical woman and South African women and highlights how the South African practice contributes to the exploitation of everyone involved, women, young men and husbands, for example, by spreading HIV/AIDS.

Diversity of African scholarship

The practitioners of African biblical interpretation are white or black Africans, Africanized scholars born outside Africa, or native Africans living on another continent. They represent a wide spectrum of ideological agendas. They may be 'liberals' fighting for LGBTQ rights or 'conservatives' who want to retain at least some traditional gender roles. There are those who think that if the text of Proverbs is liberated from the ideological agenda of white European interpretation and read from an African perspective, it will have a liberating effect (for instance, Akoto-Abutiate 2014; Kimilike

2008, 2018). Others think that a genuinely post-colonial interpretation must reveal the oppressive whiteness represented by the biblical text itself (for instance, Nel 2012; Ramantswana 2017 and some works by Masenya). There are also some who are ready to accept Western hermeneutical approaches as long as they pay due attention to issues that are pertinent in Africa (see the critique of Habtu 2010 in Nel 2012:464).

Responsibility of the interpreter

The emphasis on contextual and transformational interpretation and the process of negotiating with European methodologies and other African interpretations done from a different ideological perspective create a special awareness of the responsibility of the interpreter. African interpretations often include methodological sections that seek to develop a post-colonial hermeneutical approach to Proverbs. Questions regarding how the African context can aid understanding and to what extent and how the biblical perspectives should be subjected to ideological critique are often discussed (see, for example, Akoto-Abutiate 2014:1–30; Antwi et al. 2020:409; Masenya 2018a).

Theological interpretation

Theological interpretation is more than just reconstructing the theology of Proverbs' authors. The canonical context (of which the biblical authors were not aware) and the interpreter's theological tradition that gave birth to the canon and has been nurtured by the canon (and was, again, unknown to the biblical authors) will inform the interpretation. Here I only provide one recent example from a well-known practitioner of theological interpretation. For further, diverse examples see the selected works below.

R. W. L. Moberly's interpretation (2020) focuses on Proverbs 8, but within the context of the whole book, the Christian canon, and recent philosophical discussions. He remarks that although Proverbs 8 does not claim that God created the world by wisdom, 'the most natural [interpretive] move' (2020:27) would be to read Proverbs 8 in the light of Proverbs 3.19-20 that does make that claim. What Proverbs 8 adds is that wisdom has been with God continuously ever since the beginning of creation. That God created and has been maintaining the world by wisdom has significant consequences for the understanding of the kind of world we live in. It means that 'wisdom is in some way an intrinsic or inherent or immanent … dimension of the world' (2020:28). Consequently, 'becoming wise is a matter not just of becoming successful … but rather of being attuned to the nature of reality' (2020:33). It is the wise, that is, the righteous and just people (Proverbs 8.20), who know reality as it is. In a sense, those who become wise become a more real version of themselves because embracing reality enables people 'to be more authentically and truthfully themselves' (2020:45).

In contrast to modern philosophical discourse, in Proverbs the natural order of reality is revealed primarily through practical, relational concepts, such as trust, hope and love (see the many practical proverbs or the life of the Capable Woman in 30.10-31.31). 'The human realities of trust, hope, and love are reflections of the divine reality of the Creator, and are our best way of accessing whatever meaning there is in the world' (2020:46). Accordingly, the way to the knowledge of reality is right living. 'Learning to live rightly is an avenue to understanding' (2020:48).

The New Testament and Christian tradition, notably the Gospel of John, adopts this language and conceptuality of Proverbs to portray the Word who became flesh (John 1.1-5). The relational and creative Wisdom, according to John, is visible in the responsiveness of Jesus both to his Father and to the mundane realities of the world around him. This connection between Proverb's wisdom and Jesus suggests for the Christian that 'the reality of God as seen in Jesus is in some way an intrinsic or inherent or immanent dimension of the world. … Those who come to have faith in Jesus are not just adopting a possibly sectarian stance. … They are also in some way engaging with the true nature of the world' (2020:35).

Moberly closes with a warning to theologians. As reality is revealed through wise living,

> [p]rofessional scholars, qua scholars, have no intrinsic privilege, despite the real value of their knowledge and expertise. The challenge for (would-be) believing scholars is for their technical expertise to become attuned to this overarching and undergirding reality of the God about whom and to whom, they seek, in one way or another, to speak.'
>
> (2020:49)

This brief summary cannot do justice to the breath and depth of Moberly's argument. But it may be enough to show how his interests are not limited to reconstructing the thought of the biblical author(s). He connects Proverbs 8 with other parts of Proverbs, regardless of whether their authors knew about the work of each other. He reflects on Proverbs 8 in the light of its use in the New Testament, and in the light of Christ's life, Christian tradition and philosophical debates, none of which could have occurred to the author(s) of Proverbs. This is, however, not methodological sloppiness on Moberly's part. As he argues, 'recontextualization and intertextuality shift interpretive weight away from an author-oriented hermeneutic towards a text- and reader-oriented hermeneutic' (2020:34), which enables theological interpreters to simultaneously try to go with the grain of the text and reflect on its significance within a theological frame of reference.

Selected works

Feminist interpretation

Camp 1985, 2000; Claassens 2016; Fontaine 2002; Maier 2022; Yoder 2021

African interpretation

Golka 1993; Naré 1986; Westermann 1995 compare biblical and African proverbs.

Many articles are easily available in open-access online journals, such as:

- *OTS* (https://ote-journal.otwsa-otssa.org.za/index.php/journal)
- *HTS TSTS* (https://hts.org.za/index.php/hts)
- *Scriptura* (https://scriptura.journals.ac.za/pub/index).

The 'BlackOTBibliography' (https://ibr-bbr.org/wp-content/uploads/2020/12/BlackOTBibliography_updated.pdf) and the 'Resources for Africana Scholarship' (https://www.sbl-site.org/educational/ResourcesAntiRacism.aspx) list many relevant works.

Theological interpretation

Different theological interpretations of Proverbs are offered by Moberly (2020:13–49), Rundus (2019) and Schwáb (2013c). Some commentaries have a theological focus, such as Davis (2000) and especially Treier (2011). It is also worth checking the works of non-biblical theologians that focus on the theology of wisdom, such as Dyrness (2022) and Fiddes (2013).

Bibliography

Adamo, David T. 2015. 'Ancient Israelite and African Proverbs as Advice, Reproach, Warning, Encouragement and Explanation'. *HTS TSTS* 71(3):1–11.

Adams, Samuel L. 2008. *Wisdom in Transition: Act and Consequence in Second Temple Instructions*. Supplements to the Journal for the Study of Judaism 125. Leiden: Brill.

Ademiluka, Solomon Olusola. 2018. 'Interpreting Proverbs 22:1 in Light of Attitude to Money in African Perspective'. *OTE* 31(1):164–83.

Aitken, James K. 2007. 'Poet and Critic: Royal Ideology and the Greek Translator of Proverbs'. Pp. 190–204 in *Jewish Perspectives on Hellenistic Rulers*, edited by T. Rajak, S. Pearce, J. K. Aitken and J. Dines. Berkeley, Los Angeles, London: University of California Press.

Akoto-Abutiate, Dorothy BEA. 2014. *Proverbs and the African Tree of Life: Grafting Biblical Proverbs on to Ghanaian Eve Folk Proverbs*. Studies in Systematic Theology 16. Leiden, Boston: Brill.

Albertz, Rainer and Rüdiger Schmitt. 2012. *Family and Household Religion in Ancient Israel and the Levant*. Winona Lake: Eisenbrauns.

Albright, W. F. 1955. 'Some Canaanite-Phoenician Sources of Hebrew Wisdom'. Pp. 1–15 in *Wisdom in Israel and in the Ancient Near East*, edited by M. Noth and D. W. Thomas. Leiden: Brill.

Aletti, J. N. 1977. 'Séduction et Parole En Proverbes I-IX'. *VT* 27(2):129–44.

Alster, Bendt. 1997. *Proverbs of Ancient Sumer: The World's Earliest Proverb Collections*. Bethesda: CDL Press.

Alster, Bendt. 2005. *Wisdom of Ancient Sumer*. Bethesda: CDL Press.

Anon. n.d. 'ArtWay.Eu'. (https://www.artway.eu/artway.php?lang=en).

Ansberry, Christopher B. 2011. *Be Wise, My Son, and Make My Heart Glad*. BZAW 422. Berlin/New York: De Gruyter.

Antwi, Emmanuel K. E., Isaac F. Adjei and Joseph K. Asuming. 2020. 'Understanding Wisdom in the Old Testament through Its Akan (Ghana) Parallels: Linkages and Disconnections'. *OTE* 33(3):408–27.

Arbel, Daphna V. 1995. '"The Most Beautiful Woman," "Woman Wisdom," and "the Strange Woman": On Femininity in the Song of Songs'. Pp. 125–40 in *Poets, Prophets, and Texts in Play: Studies in Biblical Poetry and Prophecy in Honour of Francis Landy*. LHBOTS 597, edited by E. Ben Zvi, C. V. Camp,

D. M. Gunn and A. W. Hughes. London, New York, Oxford, New Delhi, Sydney: T&T Clark.

Auden, W. H. and Louis Kronenberger, eds. 1962. *The Faber Book of Aphorisms*. London: Faber and Faber Limited.

Baris, Michael. 2015. 'Iniquities Ensnare the Wicked: The Ethical Theory of Proverbs 1-9'. *HS* 56:129–44.

Barr, James. 1993. *Biblical Faith and Natural Theology*. Oxford: Clarendon Press.

Bauks, Michaela. 2015. 'Erkenntnis und Leben in Gen 2-3, Zum Wandel eines ursprünglich weisheitlich geprägten Lebensbegriffs'. *ZAW* 127(1):20–42.

Bauks, Michaela and Gerlinde Baumann. 1994. 'Im Anfang War …? Gen 1,1ff Und Prov 8, 22-31 Im Vergleich'. *Biblische Notizen* 71:24–52.

Baumann, Gerlinde. 1996. *Die Weisheitsgestalt in Proverbien 1-9*. FAT 16. Tübingen: Mohr Siebeck.

Bellis, Alice Ogden. 1996. 'The Gender and Motives of the Wisdom Teacher in Proverbs 7'. *BBR* 6:15–22.

Bellis, Alice Ogden. 2018. *Proverbs*. Wisdom Commentary 23. Collegeville: Liturgical Press.

Ben Zvi, Ehud. 2015. 'The "Successful, Wise, Worthy Wife" of Proverbs 31: 10-31 as a Source for Reconstructing Aspects of Thought and Economy in the Late Persion/Early Hellenistic Period'. Pp. 27–50 in *The Economy of Ancient Judah in Its Historical Context*, edited by M. L. Miller, E. Ben Zvi and G. N. Knoppers. Winona Lake: Eisenbrauns.

Birch, Bruce C., Walter Brueggemann, Terence E. Fretheim and David L. Petersen, eds. 2005. *A Theological Introduction to the Old Testament*. 2nd ed. Nashville: Abingdon Press.

Biri, Kudzai. 2016. 'Proverbs 31 Woman: Pentecostalism and "Disempowering Femininities" and "Oppressive Masculinities" in Zimbabwe'. Pp. 223–38 in *The Bible and Violence in Africa: Papers Presented at the BiAS Meeting 2014 in Windhoek (Namibia), with Some Additional Contributions*. BAS 20, edited by J. Hunter and J. Kügler. Magdeburg: University of Bamberg Press.

Bledsoe, Seth A. 2013. 'Can Ahiqar Tell Us Anything about Personified Wisdom?' *JBL* 132(1):119–37.

Blenkinsopp, Joseph. 1991. 'The Social Context of the "Outsider Woman" in Proverbs 1-9'. *Biblica* 72(4):457–73.

Blenkinsopp, Joseph. 1995a. *Sage, Priest, Prophet: Religious and Intellectual Leadership in Ancient Israel*. Louisville: Westminster John Knox.

Blenkinsopp, Joseph. 1995b. *Wisdom and Law in the Old Testament: The Ordering of Life in Israel and Early Judaism*. New York: Oxford University Press.

Bloom, Alfred. 1954. 'Human Rights in Israel's Thought: A Study of Old Testament Doctrine'. *Interpretation* 8(4):422–32.

Boström, Lennart. 1990. *The God of the Sages*. Stockholm: Almqvist & Wiksell.

Brown, William P. 1996. *Character in Crisis: A Fresh Approach to the Wisdom Literature of the Old Testament*. Grand Rapids: Eerdmans.

Brown, William P. 2002. 'The Pedagogy of Proverbs 10: 1-31:9'. Pp. 150–82 in *Character and Scripture: Moral Formation, Community, and Biblical Interpretation*, edited by W. P. Brown. Grand Rapids: Eerdmans.

Brown, William P. 2004. 'The Didactic Power of Metaphor in the Aphoristic Sayings of Proverbs'. *JSOT* 29(2):133–54.

Brown, William P. 2005. 'The Law and the Sages: A Reexamination of Tôrâ in Proverbs'. Pp. 251–80 in *Constituting the Community: Studies on the Polity of Ancient Israel in Honor of S. Dean BcBride Jr.*, edited by J. T. Strong and S. S. Tuell. Winona Lake: Eisenbrauns.

Brown, William P. 2014. *Wisdom's Wonder: Character, Creation, and Crisis in the Bible's Wisdom Literature*. Grand Rapids: Eerdmans.

Brown, William P. 2019. 'Rebuke, Complaint, Lament, and Praise: Reading Proverbs and Psalms Together'. Pp. 65–76 in *RPI*.

Brown, William P. 2022. 'From Rebuke to Testimony to Proverb: Wisdom's Many Pedagogies'. Pp. 433–54 in *CCBWL*.

Brueggemann, Walter. 1996. 'The Loss and Recovery of Creation in Old Testament Theology'. *Theology Today* 53:177–90.

Brueggemann, Walter. 1997. *Theology of the Old Testament*. Minneapolis: Fortress Press.

Bryce, Glendon E. 1979. *A Legacy of Wisdom: The Egyptian Contribution to the Wisdom of Israel*. Lewisburg, London: Bucknell University Press, Associated University Presses.

Budge, E. A. Wallis. 1923. 'The Admonitions of Amenemapt, the Son of Kanekht'. Pp. 9–18 in *Facsimiles of Egyptian Hieratic Papyri in the British Museum*, edited by E. A. W. Budge. London: The British Museum.

Burlingame, Andrew R. 2019. 'Writing and Literacy in the World of Ancient Israel: Recent Developments and Future Directions'. *Bibliotheca Orientalis* 76(1–2):45–74.

Byargeon, Rick W. 1997. 'The Structure and Significance of Proverbs 9: 7-12'. *JETS* 40(3):367–75.

Camp, Claudie V. 1985. *Wisdom and the Feminine in the Book of Proverbs*. Sheffield: Almond Press.

Camp, Claudie V. 2000. *Wise, Strange and Holy: The Strange Woman and the Making of the Bible*. JSOTSup 320. Sheffield: Sheffield Academic Press.

Camp, Claudie V. 2015. 'Proverbs and the Problem of the Moral Self'. *JSOT* 40(1):25–42.

Carr, David M. 2005. *Writing on the Tablet of the Heart*. Oxford: Oxford University Press.

Carr, David M. 2011. *The Formation of the Hebrew Bible: A New Reconstruction*. Oxford: Oxford University Press.

CDLI. 2015. 'Literary Descent of Ishtar' in *CDLI*.

Cezula, Ntozakhe Simon. 2017. 'The "Fear of the Lord/God" in Context of the South Africa We Pray for Campaign'. *Scriptura* 116:15–26.

Chapman, Stephen B. 2000. *The Law and the Prophets: A Study in Old Testament Canon Formation*. FAT 27. Tübingen: Mohr Siebeck.

Chebet, Dorcas and Beatrice Cherop. 2015. 'Gender and Poverty: Rereading Proverbs 31 in Pursuit of Socio-Economic Justice for Women in the Reformed Church of East Africa'. Pp. 193–218 in *Living with Dignity: African Perspectives on Gender Equality*, edited by E. Mouton, G. Kapuma, L. Hansen and T. Togom. Stellenbosch: Sun Press.

Childs, Brevard S. 1979. *Introduction to the Old Testament as Scripture*. London: SCM Press.

Claassens, L. Juliana. 2016. 'The Woman of Substance and Human Flourishing: Proverbs 31: 10-31 and Martha Nussbaum's Capabilities Approach'. *Journal of Feminist Studies in Religion* 32(1):5–19.

Clifford, Richard J. 1997. 'Observations on the Text and Versions of Proverbs'. Pp. 47–61 in *WYAMS*.

Clifford, Richard J. 1999. *Proverbs*. Louisville: Westminster John Knox.

Clifford, Richard J. 2004. 'Your Attention Please! Heeding the Proverbs'. *JSOT* 29(2):155–63.

Clifford, Richard J. 2009. 'Reading Proverbs 10-22'. *Interpretation* 63(3):242–53.

Clines, David J. A. 1974. 'The Tree of Knowledge and the Law of Yahweh (Psalm XIX)'. *VT* 24(1):8–14.

Crenshaw, James L. 1976. 'Prolegomenon'. Pp. 1–60 in *Studies in Ancient Israelite Wisdom*, edited by J. L. Crenshaw. New York: Ktav Publishing House.

Crenshaw, James L. 1998a. *Education in Ancient Israel: Across the Deadening Silence*. New York, London, Toronto, Sydney, Auckland: Doubleday.

Crenshaw, James L. 1998b. *Old Testament Wisdom: An Introduction*. Louisville: Westminster John Knox.

Crenshaw, James L. 2019. 'Wisdom Traditions and the Writings: Sage and Scribe'. Pp. 84–98 in *OHWHB*.

Davies, Graham I. 1995. 'Were There Schools in Ancient Israel?' Pp. 199–211 in *Wisdom in Ancient Israel, Essays in Honour of J. A. Emerton*. Cambridge: Cambridge University Press.

Davis, DeWayne F. 2010. *Topical Book of Proverbs: Wisdom at Your Fingertips*. Denver: Outskirts Press.

Davis, Ellen F. 2000. *Proverbs, Ecclesiastes, and the Song of Songs*. Louisville: Westminster John Knox.

Davis, Ellen F. 2019. *Opening Israel's Scriptures*. New York: Oxford University Press.

Davis, Tamie. 2022. 'Honoring a Wise Tanzanian Woman: Ufoo Kassa George's Biblie Na Utajiri (The Bible and Wealth)'. Pp. 176–90 in *Honoring the Wise: Wisdom in Scripture, Ministry, and Life; Celebrating Lindsay Wilson's Thirty Years at Ridley*, edited by J. Firth and P. A. Barker. Eugene: Wipf & Stock.

Dell, Katharine J. 2004. 'How Much Wisdom Literature Has Its Roots in the Pre-Exilic Period?' Pp. 251–71 in *In Search of Pre-Exilic Israel*, edited by J. Day. London: T&T Clark.

Dell, Katharine J. 2006. *The Book of Proverbs in Social and Theological Context*. Cambridge: Cambridge University Press.

Dell, Katharine J. 2009. 'Proverbs 1-9: Issues of Social and Theological Context'. *Interpretation* 63(3):229–40.

Dell, Katharine J. 2010. 'The Significance of the Wisdom Tradition in the Ecological Debate'. Pp. 56–69 in *Ecological Hermeneutics: Biblical, Historical and Theological Perspectives*. London: T&T Clark.

Dell, Katharine J. 2016. 'Wisdom and Folly in the City: Exploring Urban Contexts in the Book of Proverbs'. *SJT* 69(4):389–401.

Dell, Katharine J. 2019. 'Didactic Intertextuality: Proverbial Wisdom as Illustrated in Ruth'. Pp. 103–14 in *RPI*.

Dell, Katharine J. 2020. *The Solomonic Corpus of 'Wisdom' and Its Influence*. Oxford: Oxford University Press.

Dell, Katharine J. 2022. 'Theological Themes in the "Wisdom Literature": Proverbs, Job and Ecclesiastes'. Pp. 96–115 in *CCBWL*.

Dell, Katharine J. 2023. *The Theology of the Book of Proverbs*. Cambridge: Cambridge University Press.

Dell, Katharine J. and Will Kynes, eds. 2013. *Reading Job Intertextually*. New York, London: T&T Clark.

Dell, Katharine J. and Will Kynes. 2019. 'Introduction'. Pp. 1–7 in *RPI*.

Demsky, Aaron. 2014. 'Researching Literacy in Ancient Israel: New Approaches and Recent Developments'. Pp. 89–104 in *SIW*.

Doll, Peter. 1985. *Menschenschöpfung und Weltschöpfung in der alttestamentlichen Weisheit*. BSac 117. Stuttgart: Verlag Katholisches Bibelwerk GmbH.

Dyrness, William A. 2022. *The Facts on the Ground: A Wisdom Theology of Culture*. Eugene: Cascade Books.

Eissfeldt, Otto. 1913. *Der Maschal im Alten Testament*. BZAW 24. Giessen: Alfred Töpelmann.

Emerton, J. A. 2001. 'The Teaching of Amenemope and Proverbs XXII 17-XXIV 22: Further Reflections on a Long-Standing Problem'. *VT* 51(4):431–65.

Erman, Adolf. 1924. 'Eine Ägyptische Quelle Der Sprüche Salomos'. Pp. 86–93 in *Sitzungsberichte der preussischen Akademie der Wissenschaften*. SPAW 15. Berlin: Verlag der Akademie der Wissenschaften. In Kommission bei Walter de Gruyter u. Co.

Estes, Daniel J. 1997. *Hear, My Son: Teaching and Learning in Proverbs 1-9*. Downers Grove: Apollos.

Estes, Daniel J. 2010. 'What Makes the Strange Woman of Proverbs 1-9 Strange?' Pp. 151–69 in *Ethical and Unethical in the Old Testament: God and Humans in Dialogue*, edited by K. J. Dell. New York, London: T&T Clark.

Faigenbaum-Golovin, Shira. 2021. *Algorithmic Handwriting Analysis of Iron Age Documents* (https://www.youtube.com/watch?v=UOT420OTSjg).

Faigenbaum-Golovin, Shira, Arie Shaus, Barak Sober, David Levin, Nadav Na'aman, Benjamin Sass, Eli Turkel, Eli Piasetzky and Israel Finkelstein. 2016. 'Algorithmic Handwriting Analysis of Judah's Military Correspondence Sheds Light on Composition of Biblical Texts'. *Proceedings of the National Academy of Sciences* 113(17):4664–9. Doi: 10.1073/pnas.1522200113.

Farmer, Kathleen A. 1991. *Proverbs & Ecclesiastes: Who Know What Is Good?* Grand Rapids/Edingburgh: Eerdmans/The Handsel Press.

Fentress-Williams, Judy and Melody D. Knowles. 2018. 'Affirming and Contradicting Gender Stereotypes'. Pp. 137–70 in *The Hebrew Bible: Feminist and Intersectional Perspectives*, edited by G. A. Yee. Minneapolis: Fortress Press.

Fiddes, Paul S. 2013. *Seeing the World & Knowing God: Hebrew Wisdom & Christian Doctrine in a Late-Modern Context*. Oxford: Oxford University Press.

Finkelstein, Israel and Amihai Mazar. 2007. *The Quest for the Historical Israel: Debating Archaeology and the History of Early Israel*, edited by B. Schmidt. Atlanta: Society of Biblical Literature.

Fishbane, Michael. 1985. *Biblical Interpretation in Ancient Israel*. Oxford: Clarendon Press.

Fischer, Stefan. 2019. 'Foreign Women in the Book of Proverbs'. Pp. 109–23 in *Foreign Women—Women in Foreign Lands*. Oriental Religions in Antiquity 35, edited by Angelika Berlejung and Marianne Grohmann. Tübingen: Mohr Siebeck.

Fitzpatrick-mckinley, Anne. 1999. *The Transformation of Torah from Scribal Advice to Law*. JSOTSup 287. Sheffield: Sheffield Academic Press.

Fogielman, Charles-Antoine. 2019. 'Ithiel and Ucal in Prov 30:1'. *RB* 126(3):451–6.

Fontaine, Carole R. 1982. *Traditional Sayings in the Old Testament*. Sheffield: The Almond Press.

Fontaine, Carole R. 2002. *Smooth Words: Women, Proverbs and Performance in Biblical Wisdom*. London, New York: T&T Clark.

Forti, Tova L. 2007. 'The "Isha Zara" in Proverbs 1-9: Allegory and Allegorization'. *HS* 48:89–100.

Forti, Tova L. 2008. *Animal Imagery in the Book of Proverbs*. Leiden: Brill.

Forti, Tova L. 2020. 'Female Imagery in Wisdom Literature'. Pp. 177–94 in *WBCWL*.

Fox, Michael V. 1968. 'Aspects of the Religion of the Book of Proverbs'. *Hebrew Union College Annual* 39:55–69.

Fox, Michael V. 1995. 'World Order and Ma'at: A Crooked Parallel'. *Journal of Ancient Near Eastern Society of Columbia University* 23:31–48.

Fox, Michael V. 1996. 'The Social Location of the Book of Proverbs'. Pp. 227–39 in *Texts, Temples, and Traditions: A Tribute to Menahem Haran*, edited by M. V. Fox, V. A. Hurowitz, A. Hurvitz, M. L. Klein, B. J. Schwartz and N. Shupak. Winona Lake: Eisenbrauns.

Fox, Michael V. 1997. 'Who Can Learn? A Dispute in Ancient Pedagogy'. Pp. 62–77 in *WYAMS*.

Fox, Michael V. 2000. *Proverbs 1-9*. AB 18A. New Haven and London: Yale University Press.

Fox, Michael V. 2003. 'Wisdom and the Self-Presentation of Wisdom Literature'. Pp. 153–72 in *Reading from Right to Left, Essays on the Hebrew Bible in Honour of David J. A. Clines*. JSOTSup 373. London and New York: T&T Clark.

Fox, Michael V. 2004. 'The Rhetoric of Disjointed Proverbs'. *JSOT* 29(2):165–77.

Fox, Michael V. 2007. 'The Epistemology of the Book of Proverbs'. *JBL* 126(4):669–84.

Fox, Michael V. 2009. *Proverbs 10-31*. AB 18B. New Haven and London: Yale University Press.

Fox, Michael V. 2011. 'Ancient Near Eastern Wisdom Literature (Didactic)'. *Religion Compass* 5(1):1–11.

Fox, Michael V. 2014. 'From Amenemope to Proverbs: Editorial Art in Proverbs 22, 17-23, 11'. *ZAW* 126:76–91.

Fox, Michael V. 2015a. *Proverbs: An Eclectic Edition with Introduction and Textual Commentary*. Atlanta: SBL Press.

Fox, Michael V. 2015b. 'Three Theses on Wisdom'. Pp. 69–86 in *WTWT*.

Franklyn, Paul. 1983. 'The Sayings of Agur in Proverbs 30: Piety or Skepticism?' *ZAW* 95:238–52.

Frydrych, Tomáŝ. 2002. *Living under the Sun: Examination of Proverbs and Qoheleth*. VTSup 90. Leiden: Brill.

Furey, Constance M., Joel Marcus LeMon, Brian Matz, Thomas Römer, Jens Schröter, Barry Dov Walfish and Eric Ziolkowski, eds. 2009. *Encyclopedia of the Bible and Its Reception*. Berlin/Boston: De Gruyter.

Gemser, Berend. 1960. 'The Instructions of 'Onchsheshonqy and Biblical Wisdom Literature'. Pp. 102–53 in *Congress Volume Oxford 1959*. VTSup 7. Leiden: Brill.

Gerstenberger, Erhard. 1965. 'Covenant and Commandment'. *JBL* 84(1):38–51.

Gese, Hartmut. 1958. *Lehre und Wirklichkeit in der alten Weisheit*. Tübingen: Mohr Siebeck.

Gladson, Jerry Allen. 1979. *Retributive Paradoxes in Proverbs 10-29*. Ann Arbor: University Microfilms International.

Goff, Matthew. 2015. 'The Personification of Wisdom and Folly as Women in Ancient Judaism'. Pp. 128–54 in *Religion and Female Body in Ancient Judaism and Its Environments*, edited by G. G. Xeravits. Berlin, München, Boston: De Gruyter.

Goff, Matthew. 2020. 'Scribes and Pedagogy in Ancient Israel and Second Temple Judaism'. Pp. 195–212 in *WBCWL*.

Goldingay, John. 1994. 'The Arrangement of Sayings in Proverbs 10-15'. *JSOT* 19(61):75–83.

Goldingay, John. 2014. *Proverbs, Ecclesiastes and the Song of Songs for Everyone*. London: SPCK.

Goldingay, John. 2019. 'Proverbs and Isaiah 1-39'. Pp. 49–64 in *RPI*.

Golka, Friedemann W. 1983. 'Die israelitische Weisheitschule oder "des Kaisers neue Kleider."' *VT* 33(3):257–70.

Golka, Friedemann W. 1993. *The Leopard's Spots*. Edinburgh: T&T Clark.

Goswell, Gregory. 2019. 'The Ordering of the Books of the Canon and the Theological Interpretation of the Old Testament'. *JTI* 13(1):1–20.

Grabbe, Lester L. 2017. *Ancient Israel: What Do We Know and How Do We Know It?* London and New York: Bloomsbury T&T Clark.

Greenberg, Jennifer. 2017a. 'Internet Proverbs: If Solomon Had Been a Millennial'. (http://jennifergreenberg.net/2017/10/20/internet-proverbs-solomon-millennial/).

Greenberg, Jennifer. 2017b. 'Internet Proverbs, Wisdom Edition: If Solomon Had Been a Millennial'. (http://jennifergreenberg.net/2017/10/25/internet-proverbs-solomon-millennial-2/).

Grohmann, Marianne and Hyun Chul Paul Kim. 2019. 'Introduction'. Pp. 1–20 in *SWIHB*.

Habel, Norman C. 1972. 'The Symbolism of Wisdom in Proverbs 1-9'. *Interpretation* 26(2):131–57.

Habtu, Tewoldemedhin. 2010. 'Proverbs' in *Africa Bible Commentary*, edited by A. Tokunboh. Grand Rapids: Zondervan.

Hallo, William W. and K. Lawson Younger, eds. 2003. *Canonical Compositions from the Biblical World*. Vol. 1. Leiden, Boston: Brill.

Harris, Scott L. 1995. *Proverbs 1-9: A Study of Inner-Biblical Interpretation*. Atlanta: Scholars Press.

Harris, Scott L. 2000. 'Proverbs 1: 8-19,20-33 as "Introduction."' *RB* 107(2):205–31.

Hatton, Peter T. H. 2008. *Contradiction in the Book of Proverbs: The Deep Waters of Counsel*. London and New York: Routledge.

Heckl, Raik. 2015. 'How Wisdom Texts Became Part of the Canon of the Hebrew Bible'. Pp. 221–39 in *WTWT*.

van Heerden, Willie. 2002. '"The Proverb Is the Drum of God": On the Use of African Proverbs in the Interaction between African Culture and the Christian Faith'. *Scriptura* 81:462–75.

van Heerden, Willie. 2006. '"It's on the Old Mat that One Weaves the New One": The Dialogue between African Proverbs and Biblical Texts'. *OTE* 19(2):429–40.

van Heerden, Willie. 2008. 'Strategies Applied by Interpreters of the Paradox in Proverbs 26: 4-5'. *Journal for Semitics* 17:591–617.

Heim, Knut Martin. 2001. *Like Grapes of Gold Set in Silver*. Berlin: De Gruyter.

Heim, Knut Martin. 2010. 'Prov 26: 1-12:A Crash Course on the Hermeneutic of Proverb Reception and a Case Study in Proverb Performance Response'. *Die Welt des Orients* 40(2):34–53.

Heim, Knut Martin. 2013. *Poetic Imagination in Proverbs: Variant Repetitions and the Nature of Poetry*. Winona Lake: Eisenbrauns.

Hermisson, Hans-Jürgen. 1968. *Studien zur israelitischen Spruchweisheit*. WMANT 28. Neukirchen: Neukirchener Verlag.

Hildebrandt, Ted. 1988. 'Proverbial Pairs: Compositional Units in Proverbs 10-29'. *JBL* 107(2):207–24.

Hildebrandt, Ted. 1992. 'Motivation and Antithetical Parallelism in Proverbs 10-15'. *JETS* 35:433–44.

Hobgood-Oster, Laura. 2001. 'Wisdom Literature and Ecofeminism'. Pp. 35–47 in *The Earth Story in Wisdom Tradition*, edited by N. C. Habel and S. Wurst. Sheffield: Sheffield Academic Press.

Hoglund, Kenneth G. 1987. 'The Fool and the Wise in Dialogue'. Pp. 161–80 in *The Listening Heart: Essays in Wisdom and the Psalms in Honor of Roland E. Murphy, O. Carm.*, edited by K. G. Hoglund. Sheffield: Sheffield University Press.

Hrisztova-Gotthardt, Hrisztalina and Melita Aleksa Varga, eds. 2014. *Introduction to Paremiology: A Comprehensive Guide to Proverb Studies*. Warsaw/Berlin: De Gruyter.

Humphreys, W. Lee. 1978. 'The Motif of the Wise Courtier in the Book of Proverbs'. Pp. 177–90 in *Israelite Wisdom: Theological and Literary Essays in Honor of Samuel Terrien*, edited by J. G. Gammie, W. Brueggemann, W. L. Humphreys and J. M. Ward. Missoula, Montana: Scholars Press.

Hurowitz, Victor A. 2001. 'The Seventh Pillar: Reconsidering the Literary Structure and Unity of Proverbs 31'. *ZAW* 113:209–18.

Hurowitz, Victor A. 2004. 'Paradise Regained: Proverbs 3: 13-20 Reconsidered'. Pp. 49–62 in *Sefer Moshe: The Moshe Weinfeld Jubilee Volume: Studies in the Bible and the Ancient Near East, Qumran, and Post-Biblical Judaism*, edited by C. Cohen, A. Hurvitz and S. Paul. Winona Lake: Eisenbrauns.

Imray, Kathryn. 2013. 'Love Is (Strong as) Death: Reading the Song of Songs through Proverbs 1-9'. *CBQ* 75:649–65.

Janowski, Bernd. 1994. 'Die Tat Kehrt Zum Täter Zurück: Offene Fragen Im Umkreis Des 'Tun-Ergehen-Zusammenhangs'. *ZTK* 91:247–71.

Janowski, Bernd. 2013. *Arguing with God: A Theological Anthropology of the Psalms*. Louisville: Westminster John Knox.

Jones, Victoria Emily. 2015. *Art & Theology* (https://artandtheology.org/about/).

Keefer, Arthur. 2017. 'A Shift in Perspective: The Intended Audience and a Coherent Reading of Proverbs 1: 1-7'. *JBL* 136(1):103–16.

Keefer, Arthur Jan. 2020. *Proverbs 1-9 as an Introduction to the Book of Proverbs*. London, New York, Oxford, New Delhi, Sydney: T&T Clark.

Keefer, Arthur Jan. 2022. 'The Wisdom Literature and Virtue Ethics'. Pp. 455–74 in *CCBWL*.

Kimilike, Lechion Peter. 2002. 'Friedemann W. Golka and African Proverbs on the Poor'. *ZAW* 114(2):255–61.

Kimilike, Lechion Peter. 2008. *Poverty in the Book of Proverbs: An African Transformational Hermeneutic of Proverbs on Poverty*. BTA 7. New York: Lang.

Kimilike, Lechion Peter. 2018. 'Poverty Context in Proverbs 31: 1-9: A Bena Tanzanian Analysis for Transformational Leadership Training'. *OTE* 31(1):135–63.

Kipling, Rudyard. 1919. 'The Gods of the Copybook Headings' (http://www.kiplingsociety.co.uk/poems_copybook.htm).

Kirk, Alexander T. 2022. 'Toward a Reading of Proverbs 30:1b: Tracing the Life of the Text in the Versions'. *VT* 1–19.

Klawans, Jonathan. 2019. *Heresy, Forgery, Novelty: Condemning, Denying, and Asserting Innovation in Ancient Judaism*. Oxford: Oxford University Press.

Kline, Joanna Greenlee. 2021. 'Agur's Prayer (Proverbs 30: 7-9): An Everyday Response to Extraordinary Revelation'. Pp. 238–52 in *Speaking with God: Probing Old Testament Prayers for Contemporary Significance*. MBSS 8, edited by P. G. Camp and E. A. Phillips. Eugene: Wipf & Stock.

Koch, Klaus. 1955. 'Gibt Es ein Vergeltungsdogma im alten Testament?' *ZTK* 52:1–42.

Koch, Klaus. 1983. 'Is There a Doctrine of Retribution in the Old Testament?'. Pp. 57–87 in *Theodicy in the Old Testament*, edited by J. L. Crenshaw. London: SPCK.

Koptak, Paul E. 2003. *Proverbs*. Grand Rapids: Zondervan.

Kovacs, Brian. 1974. 'Is There a Class-Ethic in Proverbs?' Pp. 173–89 in *Essays in Old Testament Ethics*, edited by J. L. Crenshaw and J. T. Willis. New York: Ktav Publishing House.

Kozlova, Ekaterina E. 2021. '"Dressed as a Harlot and Cunning of Heart"? A New Look at the Heart of the Strange Woman in the Book of Proverbs'. *VT* 71(4–5):607–18.

Krispenz, Jutta. 2021. *Scribes as Sages and Prophets: Scribal Traditions in Biblical Wisdom Literature and in the Book of the Twelve*. BZAW 496. Berlin/Boston: De Gruyter.

Kselman, John S. 2002. 'Ambiguity and Wordplay in Proverbs XI'. *VT* 52(4):545–7.

Kynes, Will. 2019a. *An Obituary for 'Wisdom Literature': The Birth, Death, and Intertextual Reintegration of a Biblical Corpus*. Oxford: Oxford University Press.

Kynes, Will. 2019b. 'Wisdom Defined through Narrative and Intertextual Network: 1 Kings 1-11 and Proverbs'. Pp. 35–47 in *RPI*.

Kynes, Will. Forthcoming. 'Proverbs'. in *The New Oxford Bible Commentary*, edited by K. J. Dell and D. Lincicum. Oxford: Oxford University Press.

Lambert, W. G. 1996. *Babylonian Wisdom Literature*. Winona Lake: Eisenbrauns.

Lasater, Phillip Michael. 2019. *Facets of Fear, The Fear of God in Exilic and Post-Exilic Contexts*. Tübingen: Mohr Siebeck.

van Leeuwen, Raymond C. 1988. *Context and Meaning in Proverbs 25-27*. SBLDS 96. Atlanta: Scholars Press.

van Leeuwen, Raymond C. 1992. 'Wealth and Poverty: System and Contradiction in Proverbs'. *HS* 33:25–36.

van Leeuwen, Raymond C. 1997. 'The Book of Provers: Introduction, Commentary, and Reflections'. Pp. 17–264 in *The New Interpreter's Bible*. Vol. 5. Nashville: Abingdon Press.

van Leeuwen, Raymond C. 2007. 'Cosmos, Temple, House: Building and Wisdom in Mesopotamia and Israel'. Pp. 67–90 in *Wisdom Literature in Mesopotamia and Israel*. SBLSym 36, edited by R. J. Clifford. Atlanta: Society of Biblical Literature.

van Leeuwen, Raymond C. 2021. 'Theology: Creation, Wisdom, and Covenant'. Pp. 65–82 in *OHWB*.

Lemaire, André. 1981. *Les Écoles et La Formation de La Bible Dans l'Ancient Israël*. Göttingen: Vandenhoeck & Ruprecht.

Lemaire, André. 2001. 'Schools and Literacy in Ancient Israel and Early Judaism'. Pp. 207–17 in *The Blackwell Companion to the Hebrew Bible*, edited by L. G. Perdue. Oxford: Blackwell.

Lemaire, André. 2015. 'Levantine Literacy ca. 1000-750 BCE'. Pp. 11–45 in *CISW*.

Lenzi, Alan. 2006. 'Proverbs 8: 22-31: Three Perspectives on Its Composition'.
    JBL 125(4):687–714.
Lichtheim, Miriam, ed. 1973. *Ancient Egyptian Literature*. Oakland: University
    of California Press.
Lichtheim, Miriam. 1996. 'Didactic Literature'. Pp. 243–62 in *Ancient Egyptian
    Literature: History and Forms*, edited by A. Lopriendo. Leiden: Brill.
Lipiński, E. 1988. 'Royal and State Scribes in Ancient Jerusalem'. Pp. 157–64
    in *Congress Volume: Jerusalem 1986*. VTSup 40, edited by J. A. Emerton.
    Leiden, New York, København, Köln: Brill.
Lipschits, Oded. 2018. 'Judah under Assyrian Rule and the Early Phase of
    Stamping Jar Handles'. Pp. 337–79 in *AHEJ*.
Loader, James Alfred. 2014. *Proverbs 1-9*. Leuven – Paris – Walpole: Peeters.
Longman III, Tremper. 2006. *Proverbs*. Grand Rapid: Baker Academic.
Longman III, Tremper. 2021. 'Theology of Wisdom'. Pp. 389–406 in *OHWB*.
Lucas, Ernest C. 2015. *Proverbs*. Grand Rapids/Cambridge: Eerdmans.
Luchsinger, Jürg Thomas. 2010. *Poetik der alttestamentlichen Spruchweisheit*.
    PSAT 3. Stuttgart: Kohlhammer.
Lyu, Sun Myung. 2012. *Righteousness in the Book of Proverbs*. FAT 55.
    Tübingen: Mohr Siebeck.
Maier, Christl M. 2014. 'Good and Evil Women in Proverbs and Job: The
    Emergence of Cultural Stereotypes'. Pp. 77–92 in *The Writings and Later
    Wisdom Books, Bible and Women*, edited by C. M. Maier and N. Calduch-
    Benages. Atlanta: SBL Press.
Maier, Christl M. 2022. 'Wisdom and Women—Wisdom of Women'.
    Pp. 211–233 in *Gerhard von Rad and the Study of Wisdom Literature*. AIL 46,
    edited by Timothy J. Sandoval and Bernd U. Schipper. Atlanta: SBL Press.
Malchow, Bruce V. 1985. 'A Manual for Future Monarchs'. *CBQ* 47:238–45.
Mariottini, Claude. 2014. 'Human Rights in the Old Testament' (https://
    claudemariottini.com/2014/06/18/human-rights-in-the-old-testament/).
Masenya, Madipoane. 2015. 'In the Ant's School of Wisdom: A Holistic
    African-South African Reading of Proverbs 6: 6-11'. *OTE* 28(2):421–32.
Masenya, Madipoane. 2016. 'Searching for Affirming Notions of (African)
    Manhood in the Paean in Praise of the ʾĒšet Ḥayil? One African Woman's
    Response to Joel K. T. Biwul's Article, "What Is He Doing at the Gate?"' *OTE*
    29(2):360–9.
Masenya, Madipoane. 2017. 'Reading Proverbs 7 in the Context of Female
    "Blessers" and Sugar Mamas in South Africa'. *Scriptura* 116:120–32.
Masenya, Madipoane. 2018a. 'A Literary Figure or Patriarchal Reality?
    Reflections on the ʿēšet Hayil in Light of Depictions of Womanhood from
    Selected Yorùbá and Sotho Proverbs'. *Verbum et Ecclesia* 39(1):1–7.
Masenya, Madipoane. 2018b. 'Tamed Identities? Glimpsing Her Identity in
    Proverbs 10: 1-22:16 and Selected African Proverbs'. *HTS TSTS* 74(1):1–6.

Masenya, Madipoane. 2020. 'Wisdom from African Proverbs Meets Wisdom from the Book of Proverbs'. Pp. 464–78 in *WBCWL*.

McCreesh, Thomas P. 1985. 'Wisdom as Wife: Proverbs 31: 10-31'. *RB* 92(1):25–46.

McKane, William. 2970. *Proverbs*. London: SCM Press.

McLaughlin, John L. 2018. *An Introduction to Israel's Wisdom Traditions*. Grand Rapids: Eerdmans.

McLaughlin, John L. 2019. 'Wisdom from the Wise: Pedagogical Principles from Proverbs'. Pp. 29–54 in *Religions and Education in Antiquity: Studies in Honour of Michel Desjardins*. NBS 160, edited by A. Damm. Leiden, Boston: Brill.

Melcher, Sarah J. 2017. 'Job, Proverbs, and Ecclesiastes'. Pp. 159–87 in *The Bible and Disability: A Commentary*, edited by S. J. Melcher, M. C. Parsons and A. Yong. Waco: Baylor University Press.

Millar, Suzanna R. 2020. *Genre and Openness in Proverbs 10: 1-22:16*. Atlanta: SBL Press.

Millar, Suzanna R. 2022. 'The Multiple Genres of Wisdom'. Pp. 34–56 in *CCBWL*.

Millar, Suzanna R. Forthcoming. 'Interpretive Crossroads in Parallel Lines: Charting the Complexity of Antithetical Parallelism in Proverbs 10-22'. *Hebrew Bible and Ancient Israel*.

Miller, Cynthia L. 2003. 'A Linguistic Approach to Ellipsis in Biblical Poetry (Or, What to Do When Exegesis of What Is There Depends on What Isn't)'. *BBR* 13(2):251–70.

Miller, Douglas B. 2015. 'Wisdom in the Canon: Discerning the Early Intuition'. Pp. 87–113 in *WTWT*.

Moberly, R. W. L. 2020. *The God of the Old Testament, Encountering the Divine in Christian Scripture*. Grand Rapids: Baker Academic.

Moore, Rickie D. 1994. 'A Home for the Alien: Worldly Wisdom and Covenantal Confession in Proverbs 30.1-9'. *ZAW* 106:96–107.

Mowinckel, Sigmund. 1955. 'Psalms and Wisdom'. Pp. 205–24 in *Wisdom in Israel and in the Ancient Near East*, edited by M. Noth and D. W. Thomas. Leiden: Brill.

Mroczek, Eva. 2016. *The Literary Imagination in Jewish Antiquity*. Oxford: Oxford University Press.

Murphy, Roland E. 1998. *Proverbs*. WBC 22. Nashville: Thomas Nelson Publishers.

Na'aman, Nadav. 2015. 'Literacy in the Negev of the Late Monarchical Period'. Pp. 47–70 in *CISW*.

Nahkola, Aulikki. 2016. 'Orality and the Sage: A Word (Proverbs) to the Wise Suffices'. Pp. 56–82 in *PIW*.

Najman, Hindy and Irene Peirano Garrison. 2019. 'Pseudepigraphy as an Interpretive Construct'. Pp. 331–58 in *The Old Testament Pseudepigrapha: Fifty Years of the Pseudepigrapha Section at the SBL, Early Judaism and Its Literature*, edited by M. Henze and L. I. Lied. Atlanta: SBL Press.

Naré, Laurent. 1986. *Proverbes salomoniens et proverbes Mossi: Etude comparative à partir d'une nouvelle analyse de Pr. 25–29*. Frankfurt am Main: Peter Lang.

Nel, P. J. 1981. 'The Genres of Biblical Wisdom Literature'. *Journal of Northwest Semitic Languages* 9:129–42.

Nel, Philip. 1996. 'The Voice of Ms Wisdom: Wisdom as Intertext'. *OTE* 9(3):423–50.

Nel, Philip J. 2012. 'Trends in Wisdom Research: A Perspective from the African Continent'. *Scriptura* 111:460–1.

Newman, John Henry. 1852. 'Newman Reader – Idea of a University – Discourse 8' (https://www.newmanreader.org/works/idea/discourse8.html).

Niditch, Susan. 1996. *Oral World and Written Word: Orality and Literacy in Ancient Israel*. Louisville: Westminster John Knox.

Noegel, Scott B. 2021. *'Wordplay' in Ancient Near Eastern Texts*. ANEM 26. Atlanta: SBL Press.

Nwaoru, Emmanuel O. 2005. 'Image of the Woman of Substance in Proverbs 31: 10-31 and African Context'. *Biblische Notizen* 127:41–66.

O'Dowd, Ryan P. 2009. *The Wisdom of Torah: Epistemology in Deuteronomy and the Wisdom Literature*. FRLANT 225. Göttingen: Vandenhoeck & Ruprecht.

O'Dowd, Ryan P. 2017. *Proverbs*. Grand Rapids: Zondervan.

O'Dowd, Ryan P. 2019. 'Poetic Allusions in Agur's Oracle in Proverbs 30.1-9'. Pp. 103–19 in *Inner Biblical Allusion in the Poetry of Wisdom and Psalms*. LHBOTS 659, edited by M. J. Boda, K. Chau and B. LaNeel Tanner. London, New York, Oxford, New Delhi, Sydney: T&T Clark.

O'Kelly, Matthew A. 2022. 'Wisdom and the Fear of YHWH: Rethinking Their Relationship in Proverbs 1–9'. *JSOT* online first (https://journals.sagepub.com/doi/full/10.1177/03090892221116913).

Olojede, Funlola. 2012. 'Being Wise and Being Female in Old Testament and in Africa'. *Scriptura* 111:472–9.

Osborne, Grant R. 2006. *The Hermeneutical Spiral: A Comprehensive Introduction to Biblical Interpretation*. 2nd ed. Downers Grove: IVP Academic.

Osborne, William R. 2020. 'The Tree of Life in Proverbs and Psalms'. Pp. 100–21 in *The Tree of Life*, edited by D. Estes. Leiden, Boston: Brill.

Overland, Paul. 2022. *Proverbs*. Apollos Old Testament Commentary 15. London: Apollos.

Pemberton, Glenn D. 2005. 'The Rhetoric of the Father in Proverbs 1-9'. *JSOT* 30(1):63–82.

Penchansky, David. 2012. *Understanding Wisdom Literature: Conflict and Dissonance in the Hebrew Text.* Grand Rapids/Cambridge: Eerdmans.

Perdue, Leo G. 1994. *Wisdom & Creation, The Theology of Wisdom Literature.* Nashville: Abingdon Press.

Perdue, Leo G. 2000. *Proverbs.* Louisville: Westminster John Knox.

Perdue, Leo G. 2008. *The Sword and the Stylus: An Introduction to Wisdom in the Age of Empires.* Grand Rapids/Cambridge: Eerdmans.

Perry, Anthony T. 2008. *God's Twilight Zone: Wisdom in the Hebrew Bible.* Peabody: Hendrickson.

Plöger, Otto. 1983. *Sprüche Salomos.* BKAT 17. Neukirchen: Neukirchener Verlag.

Rad, Gerhard von. 1962. *Old Testament Theology, Vol. 1.* Edinburgh: Oliver & Boyd.

Rad, Gerhard von. 1966a. 'The Beginnings of Historical Writing in Ancient Israel'. Pp. 166–204 in *PHOE.*

Rad, Gerhard von. 1966b. 'The Joseph Narrative and Ancient Wisdom'. Pp. 292–300 in *PHOE.*

Rad, Gerhard von. 1972. *Wisdom in Israel.* London: SCM Press.

Ramantswana, Hulisani. 2017. 'Cutting and Blending Trees of Life (African Cultural Context and the Bible): A Decolonial Engagement with Akoto-Abutiate's Hermeneutic of Grafting'. *Exchange* 46:350–69.

Rendsburg, Gary A. 2016. 'Literary and Linguistic Matters in the Book of Proverbs'. Pp. 111–47 in *PIW.*

Richey, Madadh. 2021. 'The Media and Materiality of Southern Levantine Inscriptions'. Pp. 29–39 in *Scribes and Scribalism, The Hebrew Bible in Social Perspective,* edited by M. Leuchter. New York, London, Oxford, New Delhi, Sydney: Bloomsbury.

Rofé, Alexander. 2002. *Deuteronomy: Issues and Interpretation.* London: T&T Clark.

Rollston, Christopher A. 2010. *Writing and Literacy in the World of Ancient Israel: Epigraphic Evidence from the Iron Age.* ABS 11. Atlanta: Society of Biblical Literature.

Rollston, Christopher A. 2015. 'Scribal Curriculum during the First Temple Period: Epigraphic Hebrew and Biblical Evidence'. Pp. 71–101 in *CISW.*

Rollston, Christopher A. 2018. 'Scripture and Inscriptions: Eighth-Century Israel and Judah in Writing'. Pp. 457–73 in *AHEJ.*

Rotasperti, Sergio. 2021. *Metaphors in Proverbs: Decoding the Language of Metaphor in the Book of Proverbs.* VTSup 188. Leiden, Boston: Brill.

Rundus, Lance. 2019. *Wisdom Is a Woman: The Canonical Metaphor of Lady Wisdom in Proverbs 1-9 Understood in Light of Theological Aesthetics.* Eugene: Pickwick Publications.

Ryken, Leland. 2016. *Short Sentences Long Remembered: A Guided Study of Proverbs and Other Wisdom Literature*. Bellingham: Lexham Press.

Sachau, Eduard. 1911. *Aramäische Papyrus Und Ostraka Aus Einer Jüdischen Militär-Kolonie Zu Elephantine*. Leipzig: J. C. Hinrichs'sche Buchhandlung.

Sanders, Seth L. 2009. *The Invention of Hebrew*. Urbana and Chicago: University of Illinois Press.

Sanders, Seth L. 2017. *From Adapa to Enoch: Scribal Culture and Religious Vision in Judea and Babylon*. TSAJ 167. Tübingen: Mohr Siebeck.

Sandoval, Timothy J. 2006. *The Discourse of Wealth and Poverty in the Book of Proverbs*. BIS 77. Leiden: Brill.

Sandoval, Timothy J. 2007. 'Revisiting the Prologue of Proverbs'. *JBL* 126(3):455–73.

Sandoval, Timothy J. 2019. 'Prophetic and Proverbial Justice: Amos, Proverbs, and Intertextuality'. Pp. 131–51 in *SWIHB*.

Sandoval, Timothy J. 2020a. 'Text and Intertexts: A Proposal for Understanding Proverbs 30.1b'. *JSOT* 45(2):158–77.

Sandoval, Timothy J. 2020b. 'The Orality of Wisdom Literature'. Pp. 267–85 in *WBCWL*.

Scheetz, Jordan M. 2011. *The Concept of Canonical Intertextuality and the Book of Daniel*. Eugene: Pickwick Publications.

Schellenberg, Annette. 2015. 'Don't Throw the Baby Out with the Bathwater: On the Distinctness of the Sapiential Understanding of the World'. Pp. 115–43 in *WTWT*.

Schellenberg, Annette. 2018. '"May Her Breasts Satisfy You at All Times" (Prov 5:19): On the Erotic Passages in Proverbs and Sirach and the Question of How They Relate to the Song of Songs'. *VT* 68(2):252–71.

Schipper, Bernd U. 2019a. *Proverbs 1-15*. Minneapolis: Fortress Press.

Schipper, Bernd U. 2019b. '"Teach Them Diligently to Your Son!": The Book of Proverbs and Deuteronomy'. Pp. 21–34 in *RPI*.

Schipper, Bernd U. 2021. *The Hermeneutics of Torah: Proverbs 2, Deuteronomy, and the Composition of Proverbs 1-9*. AIL 43. Atlanta: SBL Press.

Schmid, Hans Heinrich. 1966. *Wesen und Geschichte Der Weisheit*. Berlin: Verlag Alfred Töpelmann.

Schmid, Hans Heinrich. 1968. *Gerechtigkeit als Weltordnung*. Tübingen: Mohr Siebeck.

Schmid, Konrad and Jens Schröter. 2021. *The Making of the Bible: From the First Fragments to Sacred Scripture*. Cambridge, Massachusetts and London, England: The Belknap Press of Harvard University Press.

Schniedewind, William M. 2004. *How the Bible Became a Book*. Cambridge: Cambridge University Press.

Schniedewind, William M. 2015. 'Scripturalization in Ancient Judah'. Pp. 305–21 in *CISW*.

Schniedewind, William M. 2019. *The Finger of the Scribe: How Scribes Learned to Write the Bible*. Oxford: Oxford University Press.

Schroer, Silvia. 2000. *Wisdom Has Built Her House*. Collegeville: The Liturgical Press.

Schwáb, Zoltán. 2013a. 'Is Fear of the Lord the Source of Wisdom or Vice Versa?' *VT* 63(4):652–62.

Schwáb, Zoltán. 2013b. 'The Sayings Clusters in Proverbs: Towards an Associative Reading Strategy'. *JSOT* 38(1):59–79.

Schwáb, Zoltán S. 2013c. *Toward an Interpretation of the Book of Proverbs, Selfishness and Secularity Reconsidered*. Winona Lake: Eisenbrauns.

Schwáb, Zoltán. 2016. 'I, the Fool: A "Canonical" Reading of Proverbs 26: 4-5'. *Journal of Theological Interpretation* 10(1):31–50.

Schwáb, Zoltán. 2022a. 'Creation in the Wisdom Literature'. in *CCBWL*.

Schwáb, Zoltán S. 2022b. 'Does the Reader Fear God for Nothing? A Theological Reflection on the Divine Speeches in Job'. *Journal of Theological Studies* 73(2):439–473.

Schweitzer, Steven. 2012. 'The Egyptian Goddess Ma'at and Lady Wisdom in Proverbs 1-9: Reassessing Their Relationship'. Pp. 113–32 in *A Teacher for All Generations: Essays in Honor of James C. VanderKam*. Vol. 1. Leiden, Boston: Brill.

Scott, Robert B. Y. 1972. 'Wise and Foolish, Righteous and Wicked'. Pp. 146–65 in *Studies in Religion of Ancient Israel*, edited by G. A. Anderson. Leiden: Brill.

Scott, Robert B. Y. 1974. *Proverbs, Ecclesiastes*. 2nd ed. Garden City, New York: Doubleday.

Seal, David. 2021. 'Proverbs through the Eyes (and Ears) of Performance'. *Scandinavian Journal of the Old Testament* 35(1):148–59.

Shapiro, Adam R. 2022. 'A God beyond Logic: The History of Natural Theology Shows that Intelligent Design and New Atheism Both Got It Wrong, in Strangely Similar Ways'. *Aeon* (https://aeon.co/essays/for-natural-theologians-proving-god-was-beside-the-point).

Shmuel, Aḥituv and Amihai Mazar. 2014. 'The Inscriptions from Tel Reḥov and Their Contribution to the Study of Script and Writing during Iron Age IIA'. Pp. 39–68 in *SIW*.

Shupak, Nili. 1993. *Where Can Wisdom Be Found? The Sage's Language in the Bible and in Ancient Egyptian Literature*. OBO 130. Göttingen: Vandenhoeck & Ruprecht.

Shupak, Nili. 2005. 'The Instruction of Amenemope and Proverbs 22: 17-24:22 from the Perspective of Contemporary Research'. Pp. 203–20 in *SOW*.

Shupak, Nili. 2011. 'Female Imagery in Proverbs 1-9 in the Light of Egyptian Sources'. *VT* 61(2):310–23.

Sinnott, Alice M. 2005. *The Personification of Wisdom*. London and New York: Routledge.

Ska, Jean Louis. 2014. 'Abraham, Maître de Sagesse Selon l'idéal Des Proverbes'. Pp. 18–29 in *Wisdom for Life: Essays Offered to Honor Prof. Maurice Gilbert, SJ on the Occasion of His Eightieth Birthday*. BZAW 445, edited by N. Calduch-Benages. Berlin: De Gruyter.

Skehan, Patrick. 1948. 'A Single Editor for the Whole Book of Proverbs'. *CBQ* 10:115–30.

Skladny, U. 1962. *Die Ältesten Spruchsammlungen in Israel*. Göttingen: Vandenhoeck & Ruprecht.

Sneed, Mark R. 2011. 'Is the "Wisdom Tradition" a Tradition?' *CBQ* 73:50–71.

Sneed, Mark R. 2015. *The Social World of the Sages: An Introduction to Israelite and Jewish Wisdom Literature*. Minneapolis: Fortress Press.

Sneed, Mark R. 2019. 'Twice-Told Proverbs as Inner-Biblical Exegesis'. Pp. 89–102 in *RPI*.

Snell, Daniel C. 1993. *Twice-Told Proverbs and the Composition of the Book of Proverbs*. Winona Lake: Eisenbrauns.

Steinberg, Julius. 2019. 'Reading Proverbs as a Book in the Writings'. Pp. 181–98 in *OHWHB*.

Stewart, Anne W. 2016. *Poetic Ethics in Proverbs: Wisdom Literature and the Shaping of the Moral Self*. New York: Cambridge University Press.

Stuart, Elizabeth. 2006. 'Proverbs'. Pp. 325–37 in *The Queer Bible Commentary*, edited by D. Guest, R. E. Goss, M. West and T. Bohache. London: SCM Press.

Tali, Education Fund. n.d. 'Visual Midrash from the Tali Education Fund'. הנומת שרדמ (http://talivirtualmidrash.org.il/en/).

Tan Nam Hoon, Nancy. 2008. *The 'Foreignness' of the Foreign Woman in Proverbs 1-9: A Study of the Origin and Development of a Biblical Motif*. Berlin/New York: De Gruyter.

Tavares, Ricardo. 2007. *Eine königliche Weisheitslehre? Exegetische Analyse von Sprüche 28-29 und Vergleich mit den ägyptischen Lehren Merikaras und Amenemhats*. OBO 234. Göttingen: Academic Press Fribourg, Vandenhoeck & Ruprecht.

The Visual Commentary on Scripture. n.d. 'Proverbs | The Visual Commentary on Scripture' (https://thevcs.org/exhibitions/old-testament/Proverbs).

Ticciati, Susannah. 2021. 'Wisdom in Patristic Interpretation: Scriptural and Cosmic Unity in Athanasius's Exegesis of Proverbs 8:22'. Pp. 187–204 in *OHWB*.

van der Toorn, Karel. 2007. *Scribal Culture and the Making of the Hebrew Bible*. Cambridge, MA; London: Harvard University Press.

Treier, Daniel J. 2011. *Proverbs & Ecclesiastes*. Grand Rapids: Brazos Press.

VanDrunen, David. 2013. 'Wisdom and the Natural Moral Order: The Contribution of Proverbs to a Christian Theology of Natural Law'. *Journal of the Society of Christian Ethics* 33(1):153–68.

Vargha, Katalin and Anna T. Litovkina. 2013. 'Punning in Hungarian Anti-Proverbs'. *European Journal of Humour Research* 1(3):15–25.

Vayntrub, Jacqueline. 2016. 'The Book of Proverbs and the Idea of Ancient Israelite Education'. *ZAW* 128(1):96–114.

Vayntrub, Jacqueline. 2019. *Beyond Orality: Biblical Poetry on Its Own Terms*. London, New York: Routledge.

Veldhuis, Niek. 2000. 'Sumerian Proverbs in Their Curricular Context'. *Journal of the American Oriental Society* 120(3):383–99.

Venter, Pieter. 2016. 'Review of James Alfred Loader "Proverbs 1–9" (Historical Commentary on the Old Testament), Peeters Leuven, 2014'. *HTS TSTS* 72(4):8. Doi: 10.4102/hts.v72i4.3385.

Viljoen, Anneke and Pieter M. Venter. 2013. 'An Exploration of the Symbolic World of Proverbs 10: 1-15:33 with Specific Reference to "the Fear of the Lord."' *HTS TSTS* 69(1):1–6.

Voorwinde, Stephen. 2012. *Wisdom for Today's Issues: A Topical Arrangement of the Proverbs*. Phillipsburg: Presbyterian and Reformed.

Waltke, Bruce K. 2004. *The Book of Proverbs: Chapters 1-15*. Grand Rapids: Eerdmans.

Waltke, Bruce K. 2005. *The Book of Proverbs: Chapters 15-31*. Grand Rapids: Eerdmans.

Waltke, Bruce K. and Ivan D. V. De Silva. 2021. *Proverbs: A Shorter Commentary*. Grand Rapids: Eerdmans.

Walton, John H. 2020. 'No Books, No Authors: Literary Production in a Hearing-Dominant Culture'. In *Write That They May Read: Studies in Literacy and Textualization in the Ancient Near East and in the Hebrew Scriptures, Essays in Honour of Professor Alan R. Millard*, edited by D. I. Block, D. C. Deuel, J. C. Collins and P. J. N. Lawrence. Eugene: Pickwick Publications.

Wax, Trevin, ed. 2018. *God's Book of Proverbs*. Nashville: LifeWay Christian Resources.

Weeks, Stuart. 1999. *Early Israelite Wisdom*. Oxford: Oxford University Press.

Weeks, Stuart. 2006. 'The Context and Meaning of Proverbs 8:30a'. *JBL* 125(3):433–42.

Weeks, Stuart. 2007. *Instruction & Imagery in Proverbs 1-9*. Oxford: Oxford University Press.

Weeks, Stuart. 2010. *An Introduction to the Study of Wisdom Literature*. London: T&T Clark.

Weeks, Stuart. 2011. 'Literacy, Orality, and Literature in Israel'. Pp. 465–78 in *On Stone and Scroll, Essays in Honour of Graham Ivor Davies*. BZAW

420, edited by J. K. Aitken, K. J. Dell and B. A. Mastin. Berlin/Boston: De Gruyter.

Weeks, Stuart. 2012. *Ecclesiastes and Scepticism*. LHBOTS 541. New York, London: T&T Clark.

Weeks, Stuart. 2015. 'Wisdom, Form and Genre'. Pp. 161–77 in *WTWT*.

Weeks, Stuart. 2016. 'The Place and Limits of Wisdom Revisited'. Pp. 3–23 in *PIW*.

Weinfeld, Moshe. 1972. *Deuteronomy and the Deuteronomic School*. Oxford: Oxford University Press.

Wendland, Kristin J. 2020. 'At Home with Wisdom: Structural Observations in Proverbs 7-9'. *Word & World* 40(3):219–26.

Westermann, Claus. 1995. *Roots of Wisdom*. Edinburgh: T&T Clark.

Westermann, Claus. 1998. *Elements of Old Testament Theology*. Atlanta: John Knox Press.

Whisenant, Jessica. 2015. 'Let the Stones Speak! Document Production by Iron Age West Semitic Scribal Institutions and the Question of Biblical Sources'. Pp. 133–60 in *CISW*.

Whybray, Norman R. 1965. *Wisdom in Proverbs*. London: SCM Press.

Whybray, Norman R. 1979. 'Yahweh-Sayings and Their Contexts in Proverbs 10: 1-22:16'. Pp. 153–65 in *La Sagesse de l'ancient Testament*. BETL 51, edited by M. Gilbert. Leuven: Leuven University Press.

Whybray, Norman R. 1982. 'Wisdom Literature in the Reign of David and Solomon'. Pp. 13–26 in *Studies in the Period of David and Solomon and Other Essays*, edited by T. Ishida. Winona Lake: Eisenbrauns.

Whybray, Norman R. 1990. 'The Sage in the Israelite Royal Court'. Pp. 133–9 in *The Sage in Israel and the Ancient Near East*, edited by J. G. Gammie and L. G. Perdue. Winona Lake: Eisenbrauns.

Whybray, Norman R. 1994a. *Proverbs*. Grand Rapids: Eerdmans.

Whybray, Norman R. 1994b. *The Composition of the Book of Proverbs*. JSOTSup 168. Sheffield: JSOT Press.

Whybray, Norman R. 1994c. 'The Structure and Composition of Proverbs 22: 17-24:22'. Pp. 83–96 in *Crossing the Boundaries: Essays in Biblical Interpretation in Honour of Michael D. Goulder*, edited by S. E. Porter, P. Joyce and D. E. Orton. Leiden: Brill.

Williams, James G. 1995. 'The Power of Form: A Study of Biblical Proverbs: Selected Studies on the Book of Proverbs'. Pp. 73–97 in *Learning from the Sages*, edited by R. B. Zuck. Eugene: Wipf & Stock.

Wilson, Lindsay. 2004. *Joseph Wise and Otherwise*. Carlisle: Paternoster.

Wilson, Lindsay. 2017. *Proverbs*. TOTC 17. Downers Grove: IVP Academic.

Wolters, Al. 2001. *The Song of the Valiant Woman: Studies in the Interpretation of Proverbs 31: 10-31*. Waynesboro: Paternoster.

Woodcock, Eldon. 1988. *Proverbs: A Topical Study*. Grand Rapids: Zondervan.

Wurst, Shirley. 2001. 'Woman Wisdom's Way: Ecokinship'. Pp. 48–64 in *The Earth Story in Wisdom Traditions*, edited by N. C. Habel and S. Wurst. Sheffield: Sheffield Academic Press.

Yee, Gale A. 1989. '"I Have Perfumed My Bed with Myrrh": The Foreign Woman ('iššâ Zārâ) in Proverbs 1-9'. *JSOT* 43:53–68.

Yee, Gale A. 2003. *Poor Banished Children of Eve: Woman as Evil in the Hebrew Bible*. Minneapolis: Fortress Press.

Yoder, Christine Roy. 2001. *Wisdom as a Woman of Substance: A Socioeconomic Reading of Proverbs 1-9 and 31: 10-31*. BZAW 304. Berlin: De Gruyter.

Yoder, Christine Roy. 2003. 'The Woman of Substance ('ešet Ḥayil): A Socioeconomic Reading of Proverbs 31: 10-31'. *JBL* 122(3):427–47.

Yoder, Christine Roy. 2005. 'Forming "Fearers of Yahweh": Repetition and Contradiction as Pedagogy in Proverbs'. Pp. 167–83 in *SOW*.

Yoder, Christine Roy. 2009a. 'On the Threshold of Kingship: A Study of Agur (Proverbs 30)'. *Interpretation* 63(3):254–63.

Yoder, Christine Roy. 2009b. *Proverbs*. Nashville: Abingdon Press.

Yoder, Christine Roy. 2019. 'Wisdom Is the Tree of Life: A Study of Proverbs 3: 13-20 and Genesis 2-3'. Pp. 11–19 in *RPI*.

Yoder, Christine Roy. 2021. 'Personified Wisdom and Feminist Theologies'. Pp. 273–86 in *OHWB*.

Young, Ian M. 1998a. 'Israelite Literacy: Interpreting the Evidence, Part I'. *VT* 48(2):239–53.

Young, Ian M. 1998b. 'Israelite Literacy: Interpreting the Evidence, Part II'. *VT* 48(3):408–22.

Young, Ian, Robert Rezetko and Martin Ehrensvärd. 2008. *Linguistic Dating of Biblical Texts*. Vol. 2. London and New York: Routledge.

Zabán, Bálint Károly. 2012. *The Pillar Function of the Speeches of Wisdom: Proverbs 1: 20-33,8: 1-36 and 9: 1-6 in the Structural Framework of Proverbs 1-9*. Berlin/Boston: De Gruyter.

Zhakevich, Philip. 2020. *Scribal Tools in Ancient Israel: A Study of Biblical Hebrew Terms for Writing Materials and Implements*. University Park, Pennsylvania: Eisenbrauns.

Zimmerli, Walther. 1964. 'The Place and Limit of the Wisdom in the Framework of the Old Testament Theology'. *SJT* 17:146–58.

Zinn, Katharina. 2018. 'Literacy in Pharaonic Egypt: Orality and Literacy between Agency and Memory'. Pp. 67–98 in *Literacy in Ancient Everyday Life*, edited by A. Kolb. Berlin/Boston: De Gruyter.

Subject Index

Biblical Reference Index